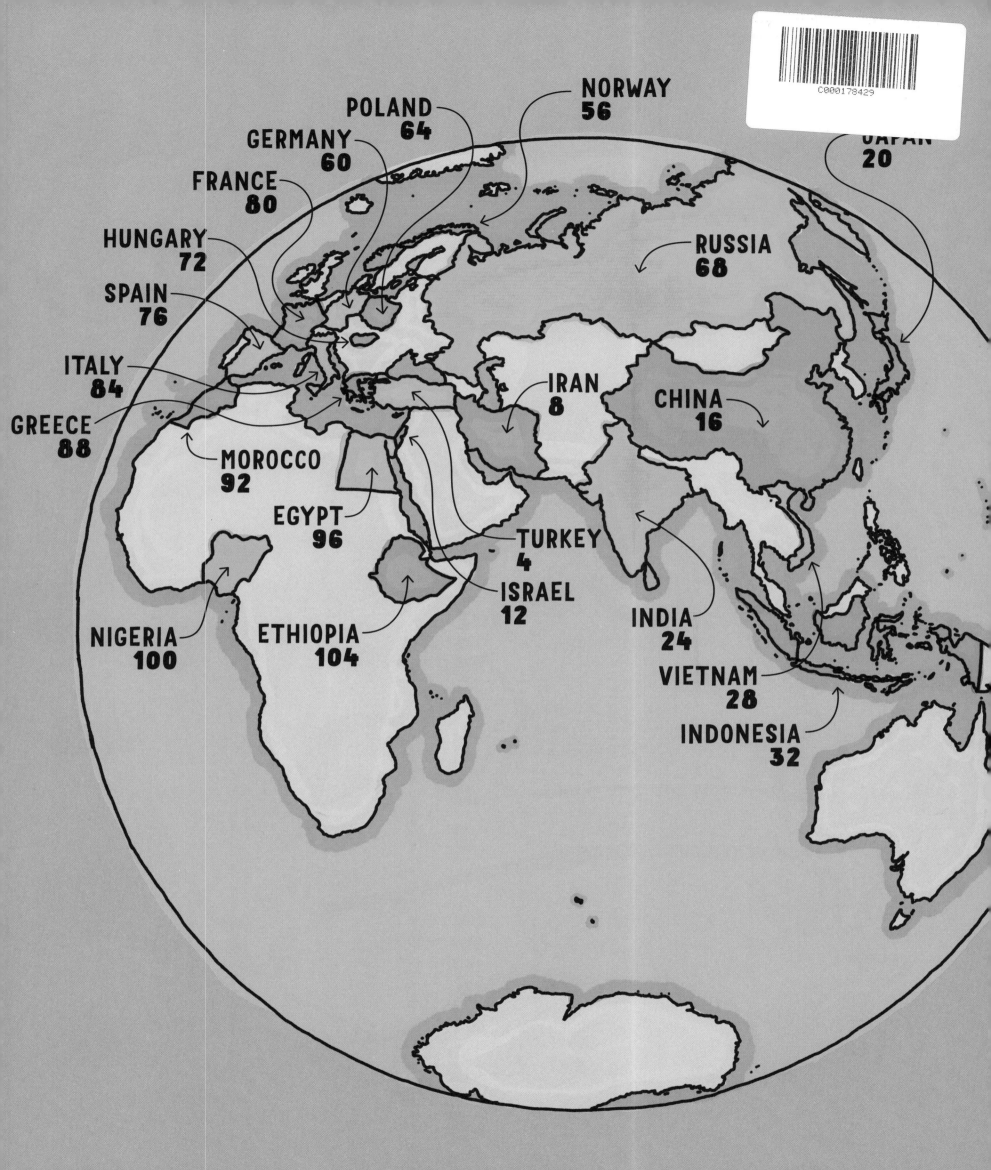

NORWAY
56

POLAND
64

GERMANY
60

FRANCE
80

HUNGARY
72

SPAIN
76

ITALY
84

GREECE
88

MOROCCO
92

EGYPT
96

NIGERIA
100

ETHIOPIA
104

JAPAN
20

RUSSIA
68

IRAN
8

CHINA
16

TURKEY
4

ISRAEL
12

INDIA
24

VIETNAM
28

INDONESIA
32

transport you instantly to a particular moment in the history of food and feasting. Finally, you'll find the **index** at the back, which puts the main ingredients used in this book right at your fingertips.
► We've done our best to pack in as much information as possible, but even if

we had 1,000 pages to fill, it wouldn't ever be enough. So, we've put together a broad selection of countries and cuisines, with an overview of their culinary traditions — from classic dishes to lesser-known, but equally tasty titbits. When it comes to recipes that are

popular in more than one country, they are only included once. In other words, this book is meant to serve as a mere introduction to the incredible history of food through the ages — and to sharpen our readers' appetites for further culinary adventures!

RECIPES

A glass is 250 ml.

4
IMAM BAYILDI
Stuffed aubergine
TURKEY

6
KAYMAKLI KAYISI TATLISI
Kaymak-stuffed apricots
TURKEY

8
TACHIN MORGH
Upside-down rice and chicken casserole
IRAN

10
KUKU SABZI
Fluffy omelette with fresh herbs
IRAN

13
HAMANTASHEN
Poppyseed-filled butter biscuits
ISRAEL

14
HUMMUS
Chickpea spread
ISRAEL

17
MAPO TOFU
Tofu in a spicy sauce
CHINA

18
CONGEE
Rice porridge
CHINA

21
MISO SOUP
An umami-flavoured soup
JAPAN

22
ONIGIRI
Rice balls
JAPAN

24
MILK BARFI
Creamy snack bar
INDIA

26
RAJMA CHAWAL
Spicy beans and rice
INDIA

28
BÁNH XÈO
Crispy stuffed crêpes
VIETNAM

30
BÁNH CHUỐI NƯỚNG
Banana cake
VIETNAM

32
OPOR AYAM
Chicken in coconut sauce
INDONESIA

35
GADO GADO
Salad with peanut sauce dressing
INDONESIA

37
HAMBURGER
Minced beef patty
UNITED STATES OF AMERICA

39
PEANUT BUTTER PIE
A creamy peanut dessert
UNITED STATES OF AMERICA

40
TACOS
Folded stuffed tortillas
MEXICO

41
TOMATO SALSA
A spicy, tangy dip
MEXICO

42
GUACAMOLE
Avocado dip
MEXICO

42
TORTILLA
Round flatbread
MEXICO

44
PAPAS RELLENAS
Potato croquettes
PERU

45
SALSA CRIOLLA
Onion garnish
PERU

46
ALFAJORES
Sandwiched cookies
PERU

49
PÃO DE QUEIJO
Cheese bread
BRAZIL

50
BRIGADEIRO
Chocolate truffles
BRAZIL

52
CARBONADA CRIOLLA
Beef and vegetable stew with fruit
ARGENTINA

55
CHOCOTORTA
Layered chocolate cake
ARGENTINA

57
KJØTTKAKER MED BRUN SAUS
Meatballs in brown sauce
NORWAY

59
TILSLØRTE BONDEPIKER
Layered apple trifle
NORWAY

60
KÄSESPÄTZLE
Cheesy drop noodles
GERMANY

TAKE A BITE

EAT YOUR WAY AROUND THE WORLD

ALEKSANDRA MIZIELIŃSKA ★ DANIEL MIZIELIŃSKI ★ NATALIA BARANOWSKA

63
KARTOFFELSALAT
Potato salad
GERMANY

64
BUCKWHEAT AND CHEESE PIEROGI
Stuffed dumplings
POLAND

67
HONEY GINGERBREAD
Cookies
POLAND

69
BLINI
Buckwheat pancakes
RUSSIA

70
KISSEL
Fruit dessert
RUSSIA

72
LECSÓ
Tomato pepper stew
HUNGARY

74
MEGGYLEVES
Sour cherry soup
HUNGARY

76
TORTILLA DE PATATAS
Potato onion omelette
SPAIN

78
GAZPACHO
Chilled tomato soup
SPAIN

81
CROQUE MONSIEUR
Ham and cheese toastie
FRANCE

82
MILLE-FEUILLE
Layered pastry dessert
FRANCE

84
TAGLIATELLE ALLA BOLOGNESE
Pasta with tomato-meat sauce
ITALY

86
PIZZA
Tomato and mozzarella pizza
ITALY

88
AVGOLEMONO SOUP
Chicken broth with egg and lemon
GREECE

91
MELOMAKARONA
Festive honey biscuits
GREECE

93
SEFFA
Sweet couscous
MOROCCO

94
BASTILLA
A sweet and savoury chicken pie
MOROCCO

96
HAWAWSHI
Meat-filled pita bread
EGYPT

98
UMM ALI
Bread pudding
EGYPT

101
GROUNDNUT SOUP
Nutty chicken stew
NIGERIA

102
JOLLOF
Slow-cooked rice
NIGERIA

104
INJERA
Flatbread
ETHIOPIA

106
DORO WAT
Stew with chicken and eggs
ETHIOPIA

107
BERBERE
Spice mixture
ETHIOPIA

TURKEY
CROSSROADS OF CULTURE

Chieftain of the Turkish tribes of Asia

Bumin Kagan

► Turkey's location means it links Europe, Asia, African and the Arab world. For centuries, this region endured attacks from the great Roman and Persian armies. Trading caravans also came from every direction. All this meant the customs and cuisines of many nations combined and created the unique traditions of modern-day Turkey.

► In the 4th century CE, the Roman emperor Constantine the Great established the capital of the Byzantine Empire in the region. It was named Constantinople in his honour.

► In the 11th century CE, nomadic tribes from Central Asia ❶ invaded southwestern Asia and formed the Seljuk dynasty ❺.

► Four centuries later, the Turks created the Ottoman Empire, a medieval superpower. They occupied a huge area that stretched between the Mediterranean and the Red and Black Seas. The empire was a mixture of Balkan, Arab and Asian traditions. The captured city of Constantinople changed its name to Istanbul, and the Turks built the magnificent Topkapı Palace ⓯ in the centre.

*See more about Constantine on page 90.

NOVEL IDEAS

► The Byzantine Empire was important politically and culturally, and it also became famous for its food. The variety of goods and ingredients that flowed in from around the world meant it was the place where new

DRIED MEAT

MUSTARD

IMAM BAYILDI
Stuffed aubergines
Soak aubergines for: 🕐 30 minutes
Preparation time: 🕐🕐 100 minutes, 3×🍽

 3 medium aubergines

 1 lemon

⅓ cup olive oil (85 ml)

2 small onions

2 garlic cloves

 2 large handfuls of parsley

4 medium tomatoes
or 2 cans chopped tomatoes (400 g each)

1 tsp cumin powder

½ tsp cinnamon

½ tsp sugar

salt and pepper to taste

yoghurt to garnish

🍆 The literal translation of *imam bayildi* is 'the imam fainted'. While it might be assumed the imam, or holy man, was overcome by the glorious taste of this dish, some believe his fainting was instead due to the cost involved. Aubergines tend to absorb quite a lot of olive oil when they are fried or braised, making this a rather pricey recipe!

1 Wash the aubergines and peel their skin to create a stripy pattern. Place them in a big bowl and cover with water. Add a teaspoon of salt and the juice of one lemon. Place a plate over the bowl and leave for 30 minutes. Rinse the aubergines and then pat dry.

2 Heat the oil in a pan, and when hot, fry the aubergines whole.

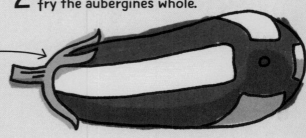

MIRACLE DIET

► In Ancient Greece, and later in Byzantium and other major parts of the medieval world, it was believed that a person's health, mood and well-being depended on the balance between four **humours**. These humours were represented by the fluids contained within the body: blood, yellow bile, phlegm and black bile.

► It was believed that what we eat could help balance the four fluids. Eating the right foods was therefore seen as a way to avoid or treat various illnesses.

For your runny nose, I recommend the warming and drying effects of honey.

Sir, you should stop eating meat.

You should add aniseed to everything you eat.

Sir, you should only be having figs in the summer — and seasoned with just salt!

dishes and flavours came alive. Byzantium became famous for its delicacies and the rest of the world picked up on these innovative recipes and did their best to replicate them.
▶ Traditionally, all types of fish and seafood were eaten, along with roasted venison, poultry and dried meats. Dishes were seasoned mainly with saffron, rosemary, aniseed, rose petals and aromatic oils.
▶ For those with a sweet tooth, there were culinary delights made with honey, cane sugar or dates. Spiced with cardamom and other flavours, these puddings, desserts, marmalades 21, jams 22 and candied fruits 13 were just the start of the region's honeyed history.

BOTTARGA
Dried and salt-cured fish roe

CAVIAR
Salt-cured fish eggs

GARUM
Fish sauce used for seasoning

ROASTED PORK IN WINE AND HONEY

GREEN PEA PUREE

CANDIED FRUITS

ORANGE MARMALADE

ROSE SUGAR

Flip them over from time to time and fry for 10–15 minutes, until they are golden.

3 Cut the onion into fine strips, dice the garlic and parsley. Peel the tomatoes and chop into small squares (unless you are using chopped tomatoes).

4 Remove the aubergines from the pan, reduce the heat and add the onion to the remaining olive oil. Fry the onion for 10 minutes, until it is soft. Add garlic, cumin and cinnamon and fry for another 3 minutes, stirring often.

5 Add the tomatoes, parsley, salt, sugar and pepper. Mix the ingredients together and cook for 10 minutes, until most of the liquid has evaporated.

6 Once the aubergines have cooled, cut into them lengthwise, but be careful not to cut all the way through. Open them up and place on top of the vegetables. Cover with a lid.

7 Heat the oven to 180°C. Arrange the aubergines in a dish. Sprinkle the insides with salt and fill with sauce.

8 Garnish with parsley and a dollop of yoghurt.

Elif absolutely adores aubergines.

MEATY SUCCESS IN THE WEST
▶ The kebab is a popular food across the entire Middle East. While there are many different types 10 17 20 the **döner kebab** is the fast-food favourite that has been adopted worldwide.
▶ The kebab was originally an Ottoman invention and was exported to the rest of the world by Turkish immigrants. Turks who arrived in Germany half a century ago set up kebab shops. By sharing a taste of their homeland they were able to make a living, and hungry Germans were soon lining up for a bite of the now famous kebab sandwich.

* Find out more about fast food on page 37.

1 Arrange meat slices on the spit.

2 Slowly roast the meat on all sides.

3 Cut thin slices of the browned outer layers.

(15) TOPKAPI PALACE

GRAINS FROM THE CRESCENT

▶ The cultivation of **wheat** began nearly 12,000 years ago in the region in the Middle East that is known as the **Fertile Crescent**. This is where the first farmers began to cultivate crops and the first human settlements were recorded. One of the earliest agricultural sites discovered is located in a region that is part of Turkey today.

▶ 2,000 years later, wheat made its way to modern-day Greece and then further west to the rest of Europe, and eastwards towards India.

▶ There are hundreds of varieties of wheat. Some are used to make pasta and grain dishes (such as bulgur ⑱), and others for bread and cakes.

ASIA

MODERN TURKEY

MEDITERRANEAN SEA

FERTILE CRESCENT

PERSIAN GULF

AFRICA

ARABIAN PENINSULA

THIN AS AIR

▶ How do you bake bread without an oven? Over 1,000 years ago, nomadic Turks had to find a solution to this quandary. Over their long voyages, they would prepare a type of bread made of many fine layers of dough, which they would fry in a pot ❷❸.

▶ A few hundred years later, the master bakers at the Topkapı Palace would replicate this method — this time not out of necessity, but purely out of culinary fancy. They stretched unbelievably thin layers of dough out to create the bread known as **yufka**❾. They spread melted butter over each layer and stacked one on top of the other, creating the sweet and savoury pastries known as baklava and börek.

BAKLAVA ⑭㉓
Layers of yufka pastry filled with crushed nuts and covered in honey or syrup.

BÖREK ⑯⑲
Layered pastry prepared with a variety of savoury fillings.

Outside of Turkey, yufka is often compared to Greek-style filo.

KAYMAKLI KAYISI TATLISI

Kaymak-stuffed apricots. Soak overnight. Preparation: 🕐 30 minutes, 25 × 🍽

250 g dried apricots

1½ cups water (375 ml)

¾ cups sugar (150 g)

2 tbsp lemon juice

160 g mascarpone or Greek yoghurt

2 handfuls of pistachio nuts or walnuts

1 handful of flaked almonds

1 tbsp melted butter

The Öztürk family enjoys this sweet apricot treat at least once a week.

TO EACH THEIR OWN

▶ While 'halva' (also written as 'halwa') is famous for being a sweet sesame-infused treat, there are a lot of different kinds ⑥ ⑦ ⑧ ⑪ ⑫. The traditional ones come from the Middle East but when these recipes migrated to Central Asia and India, new flavours were developed.

▶ Over 1,000 years ago, halva was already known as a sugary food made of sweetened wheat ④. It wasn't until later that the sesame version was devised*. Then came the rest: nutty, fruity... and even eggy!

* See more about sesame on page 15.

PIŞMANIYE ⑫

Traditional Turkish halva made from threads of sugar and flour.

HALVA ⑪

A popular form of sesame halva originating in Israel, Lebanon, Syria, Iraq and Jordan.

XALWO (also: Xalwad or Halwad)

Somalian halva made of corn flour, seasoned with cardamom and nutmeg.

GAJAR KA HALWA

Indian halva made with grated carrots.

KOZHIKODAN HALWA

Halva from the Kerala region of India, made of wheat flour.

BUTER HALUA (also booter halwa)

Chickpea-based halva from Bangladesh.

HOLWAH TAMAR

Iraqi halva made with dates.

The word 'halva' comes from the Arabic word 'hulw' meaning 'sweet'.

🍮 The name of this Turkish sweet treat means 'dessert of apricots with kaymak'. Kaymak is a thick, rich cream. If you can't find it, use mascarpone or extra-thick yoghurt instead.

1 Soak the apricots in water overnight.

2 The next day, pour the excess water from the apricots into a pot. If there is less than a glass, add more water. Bring to the boil and add the sugar, lemon juice and the apricots.

3 Boil the apricots for 10–15 minutes, then set aside to cool.

4 During cooking, the apricots should have opened up. If not, use a knife to cut them open. Fill each apricot with a spoonful of mascarpone or yoghurt.

5 Sprinkle with some pistachios or other nuts.

6 Drizzle the apricots with a few teaspoons of the syrup from the pot, some butter and sprinkle with flaked almonds.

IRAN
SHIMMERING SAFFRON, GOLD AND DATES

PERSEPOLIS   ANCIENT CAPITAL   OF PERSIA

Cyrus the Great
King of Persia

▶ Iran, formerly known as Persia, has a remarkable history. Cyrus the Great (also called Cyrus II) ❺ founded the Persian empire over 2,500 years ago. While conquests and trade meant pomegranates, rosewater and saffron spread throughout the world, in turn Persia welcomed rice, aubergines and lemons from the Far East.

▶ Persian cuisine is known as being luxurious: meat glazed in a saffron-tinted marinade and ceremonial dishes sprinkled with flakes of real silver and gold.

▶ Persia saw many rulers and dynasties, including the conquest by the king of Macedonia, Alexander the Great[1]. In the Middle Ages, Persia was ruled by Arabs but its people retained their language, customs and culinary traditions.

▶ While a dinner table in Iran might feature many traditional Middle Eastern dishes such as kebabs ㉔, stuffed breads and baklava[2] ⑬, they are likely to be paired with unique Persian dishes such as saffron rice, sour soup and fruit-based sauces.

[1] Find out more on Alexander the Great on page 96.
[2] See more on baklava on page 6.

TAHCHIN MORGH ⑩⑳
Upside-down rice and chicken casserole
Chicken prep time: ◉ 60 minutes
Roasting time: ◉ 60 minutes
Initial prep time: ⏱ 30 minutes, 4× 🍚

🧅 1 onion	🍗 1 kg chicken (preferably legs and thighs)	⦁⦁ several allspice berries
🥤🥤 1½ cups rice (270 g), preferably basmati		🌿 a pinch of saffron
🥚 2 eggs	🥤 1 cup thick yoghurt (250 ml), plus extra for garnish	▲ ¼ tsp ground turmeric ▲ ¼ tsp ground cinnamon
▲ ¼ tsp ground cumin	▲ ¼ tsp ground nutmeg	▲ ¼ tsp ground cardamom
🧈 2 tbsp butter (30g)	〰 2 tbsp soaked raisins	▲ salt to taste

1 Cut the onion into chunks and place in a pot with the chicken, salt and allspice. Cover with water and cook for an hour, until the meat is soft.

2 Take the chicken out of the pot to cool and cut into chunks. Set the broth aside.

3 Put the rice into the pot and cover with cold water. Stir vigorously with your hand, rinse out the water and repeat until the water runs clear.

4 Bring 4 cups of salted water to the boil (use 2 tsp of salt). Add the rice and boil for 5-8 minutes until the grains are cooked but still firm. Rinse with cold water and set aside to cool.

The peeled seeds are juicy and tart.

Hard, inedible exterior

White, bitter membrane within

HIDDEN TREASURES

▶ Getting through the tough skin and membrane of a **pomegranate** to extract its juicy seeds may be a challenge ❷❹⑭ but the sweet-and-tart taste of its juicy seeds has made it one of the most popular fruits in Persia for 5,000 years. Pomegranates were among the first fruits to be domesticated by humans — alongside figs, grapes, dates and olives.

▶ Pomegranates originated in Persia and then made their way to Egypt, Greece (they even got a shout-out from the Greek poet Homer*) and other Mediterranean nations.

▶ Trade took pomegranates to Asia while Spanish colonial fleets brought it to the Americas.

* Read up on Homer on page 91.

5 Crush the saffron with your fingers. Pour 3 tablespoons of boiling water over it and stir.

6 Beat the eggs in a large bowl and combine with the yoghurt. Add the saffron, turmeric and a teaspoon of salt. Add half the rice and mix again.

7 Combine the cinnamon, cumin, nutmeg and cardamom and then add the mixture to the rest of the rice, stirring well.

8 Heat the oven to 180°C. Melt the butter in a pan and use to it grease a casserole dish from top to bottom (leave a bit of butter for later). The dish should be made of glass and include a lid, preferably 24cm x 24cm.

9 Place the mixture of rice, yoghurt and eggs at the bottom, then add a layer of chicken. Sprinkle over the raisins and then add the spiced rice on top. Use a large spoon to compress all the ingredients, then add ½ cup of broth and the rest of the melted butter.

10 Cover with the lid and bake for one hour — or until the rice begins to brown from below and on the sides.

11 Wait a few minutes for the dish to cool, then use a knife to scrape the rice from the sides. Serve with yoghurt.

Ali always reaches for the most generous portion of tahchin morgh.

FAITHFUL FASTING

▸ Islam, the most common religion in Iran, has a great influence on food. Here, and in other Arabic countries, foods are split up into those that are allowed (**halal**) and those that are forbidden (**haraam**).

▸ Muslims observe a month of fasting and prayer known as **Ramadan**, when they refrain from eating from sunrise to sunset. The fasting period lasts between 29–30 days.

▸ As there are no limits on what can be eaten between dusk and dawn, each region of the Islamic world has its own snacks, dishes and drinks that are served after the evening prayer.

DATES

SHOLEH ZARD
Saffron rice pudding

ASZ
Thick soup

HALIM
Wheat and meat porridge

SWEETS
Baklava, halva, dried fruits

PRECIOUS PETALS

▸ Persians began cultivating **roses ❼** several thousand years ago. The petals were traditionally distilled into rose water, made into jam or used as decoration.

▸ Mass production, together with the deft skills of Persian merchants, meant **rose water ❽** became popular in Asia. When the Crusaders* arrived back in Europe after the Holy Wars, they brought rose water with them.

▸ Today, rose water is added to puddings and desserts.

*Refers to wars fought between Christians and Muslims over the Holy Land (currently the territory of Israel and Palestine).

GOLD STANDARD

▸ It takes about 150,000 blossoms of **saffron ❶** to prepare about 2.5 pounds of saffron, the most expensive spice in the world. Each saffron blossom contains three delicate threads known as 'stigmas', which are removed and dried (the rest of the flower is discarded). These dried threads are what is known around the world as saffron ❻. Persians have been producing, exporting and cooking with saffron for over 2,500 years.

stigmas

TEHRAN, CAPITAL OF IRAN

DIVINE DECEPTION

► **Almonds** 16 have been grown in the Middle East, including Iran, for thousands of years. These nuts then became popular in Europe in the Middle Ages. When Christian knights travelled to the Middle East during the Crusades, Arabs from Persia taught them how to prepare **almond milk** 12.

► Christians used to have very strict rules during Lent. All animal products, including cow's milk, were forbidden, so almond milk was especially handy during this period.
► This simple invention had already been adopted by Muslims for their own fasting holiday of Ramadan.

FRUIT OF THE ALMOND TREE — The almond is hidden inside the shell.

CHAGHALEH BADOOM 18 — Young almonds sprinkled with sea salt are a popular snack in Iran.

MARZIPAN 15 — A sweet treat made from roasted and ground almonds.

GREEN PLENTY

► **Pistachios** 5 17 are native to Afghanistan, but they were brought to Persia at least 9,000 years ago.
► These nuts were introduced to Europe by Alexander the Great, along with other spoils of war.

► At first pistachios were only enjoyed by the rich, but today they are widely available snacks. They are used in many dishes and are key ingredient in pistachio ice cream.

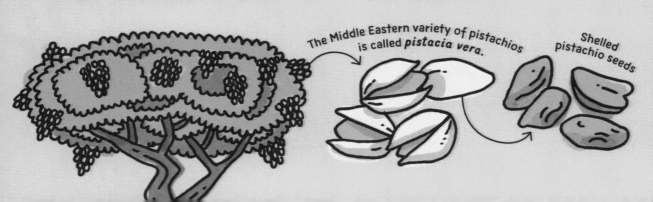

The Middle Eastern variety of pistachios is called *pistacia vera*.

Shelled pistachio seeds

KUKU SABZI
Fluffy omelette with fresh herbs
🕐 30 minutes, 1× ◎

 ⅓ cup dill

 ⅓ cup coriander

 ⅓ cup chives

⅓ cup parsley

a handful of walnuts

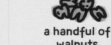 3 eggs

½ tsp salt

¼ tsp tumeric

¼ tsp cumin

1 Wash and dry the herbs. Cut the stems and finely chop the leaves.

2 In a small pan, roast the walnuts until they are browned. Once cooled, chop into chunks.

3 In a big bowl, whisk the eggs, then add salt, turmeric, cumin and baking powder. Mix well.

4 Add the chopped herbs, walnuts and cranberries and stir.

¼ tsp baking powder

a pinch of chilli powder

freshly ground pepper

2 tsp dried cranberries

3 tbsp olive oil

'Sabzi' is the Persian word for herbs. You can switch up the herb combination as you like or use different types of greens — for example, spinach (native to Persia and cultivated in the region for over 1,700 years).

Zahra makes kuku for her kids every Thursday.

5 In a small pan, heat 3 tablespoons of olive oil. Pour in the egg mix and smooth the top. Cover the pan and lower the heat. Fry for 8 to 10 minutes, until the middle is cooked.

6 Cover the pan with a flat plate and turn upside down. Using the plate, slide the omelette back into the pan, fried side up. Continue frying with the plate covering the pan for several minutes.

7 Place the kuku onto the plate and allow to cool. Cut into triangles. Serve with yoghurt or bread.

SWEET INDULGENCE

Dates 9 19 most likely come from the Fertile Crescent*. The warm and dry climate meant that they could easily be grown by early farmers of Mesopotamia and Egypt.

- These sweet and nutritious fruits proved popular and were enjoyed by everyone from the Ancient Romans to the Chinese and the medieval lords of Europe.
- Dates can be eaten on their own or added to sweet and savoury dishes. Dates are an important part of the daily diet of those living in hot desert regions.

* Find out more about the Fertile Crescent on page 6.

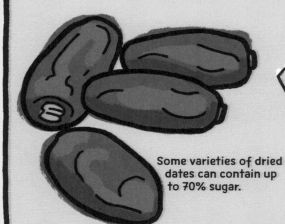

Some varieties of dried dates can contain up to 70% sugar.

Dates grow in clusters of about 1,000 individual dates and these clusters can weigh up to 10 kilograms.

In the wild, date palms can grow up to 30 metres tall, so collecting fruit can be dangerous. On plantations, date palms are often pruned before they reach 15 metres.

FLUFFY PERFECTION

- **Rice** appeared on Persian dinner tables as far back as antiquity. It came from India and China*, and over time, thanks to the unique three-stage preparation method, it became a staple of many local dishes.
- The grains are first soaked in cold water for a long time, then briefly boiled and finally steamed until tender.
- Rice prepared in this way is light and fluffy and does not stick, achieving the pinnacle of Persian splendour when seasoned with butter and saffron.

* Find out more about the history of rice on page 19.

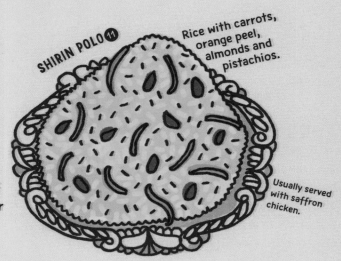

SHIRIN POLO 11

Rice with carrots, orange peel, almonds and pistachios.

Usually served with saffron chicken.

ISRAEL
FAITH AND TRADITION ALIGNED

- For Jewish people, Israel is believed to be the Promised Land given to Abraham by God. Around 3,000 years ago, the first Jewish leaders ❷ established the Kingdom of Israel and Judea, which fell to the Assyrian and Babylonian powers 300 years later ❺.
- Over the centuries, many nations attempted to take over Israel, including the Persians ❼ ⓰, Macedonians ❾ and Romans ⓫ ⓭. The Jewish people had to continuously fight to defend their rights to the territory and were often exiled from Israel. There were later invasions by Arab nations ⓲, Crusaders from Europe ⓴ and Ottoman Turks ㉒.
- Exiled Jews brought food from home, including wheat ❿, chickpeas ❻, figs ❽, dates ⓯, pomegranates ❹, grapes ⓮, olives ⓱ and olive oil ❶, as well as flatbreads ⓬, goats ❸, sheep ⓳ and cheese ㉑.
- The Jewish people's dream of establishing their own nation came true in 1948 due to an accord brokered by the British colonial powers in Palestine ㉓.
- The settlers who flowed into the new nation of Israel brought with them flavours and ingredients from the lands of their exile. From the former Ottoman Empire came samosas ㉜, pastries made of yufka ㉞*, yoghurt ㊱, couscous ㉟, pita bread ㉛, stuffed vegetables ㉕, rice ㉝ and bulgur dishes.
- From Central and Western Europe came schnitzels ㉚, strudels ㉖, herring ㉔, carp ㉘, borscht and chicken broth.
- From Arabian cuisine came falafels ㉙, hummus ㉗, shakshuka, za'atar and fresh fruit ㊲.
- Today, Israel is a spectacular mosaic of cultures and delicacies.

* More on page 6.

KOSHER

Certain types of fowl

Mammals with cloven hoofs that chew their own cud

Fish with scales and fins

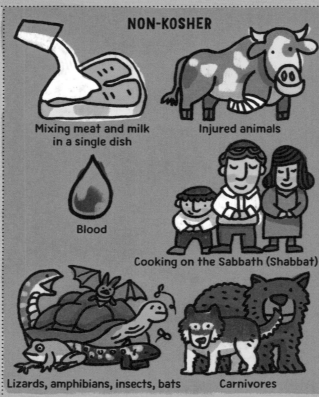

NON-KOSHER

Mixing meat and milk in a single dish

Injured animals

Blood

Cooking on the Sabbath (Shabbat)

Lizards, amphibians, insects, bats

Carnivores

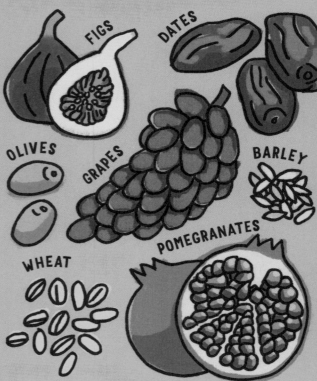

FIGS

DATES

OLIVES

GRAPES

BARLEY

WHEAT

POMEGRANATES

FORBIDDEN FOODS
- In Judaism, as in many other religions, there are rules about what foods are permitted and how these foods should be prepared.
- The principles of **kashrut**, or **kosher**, are not always clear. Rabbis* today debate the interpretation of these rules. For example, in 2008 giraffes were recognised as kosher.
- Even though there are many Jewish people who don't strictly follow the rules of kashrut, this system still has a significant impact on the types of foods that Israelis eat.

* A rabbi is the spiritual leader of a community of religious Jews.

SUPER 7
- The ancient Hebrew text of the Old Testament lists **seven types** of plants that are considered quintessential to Israeli cuisine. These two grains and five fruits still hold a principal spot in the hierarchy of Jewish culinary tradition.

BASIC BREAD

► Aside from the rules of kashrut, other aspects of Judaism also have an influence on the food Israelis eat.

► Passover (**Pesach**) is one of the oldest Jewish holidays. Lasting over a week, it celebrates the Israelites escaping enslavement in Egypt. During Passover, Jewish people are not allowed to eat or store **chametz** — foods that have been leavened or use leavening agents*, including risen dough, or fermented drinks produced from grains.

► The only exception to this rule is **matzo**, which is a wheat cracker made of just flour and water. Its simplicity represents the terrible conditions faced by enslaved Jewish people on their journey out of Egypt. During Passover, it is eaten at every meal and is used to make soup noodles or to thicken other dishes.

* More on page 97.

HAMANTASHEN
Poppyseed-filled butter biscuits
Preparation: ⏱ 30 minutes, chill for: ⏱ 1 hour, bake for: ⏱ 25 minutes, 25×▲

 1¼ cups flour (180 g) plus extra for sprinkling

 a pinch of salt

 1 orange

 90 g butter at room temperature

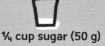 ¼ cup sugar (50 g)

 2 eggs, plus 1 for extra glazing

 ½ tsp vanilla extract Or ½ pod of vanilla beans

 ⅓ can poppyseed paste (150 g)

As per tradition, these biscuits are typically filled with a poppyseed paste. However, there are variations that include fruit fillings. So, if you can't get your hands on poppyseed, feel free to use marmalade instead.

Press the edges down firmly.

1 Sift the flour into a bowl. Add a pinch of salt and mix.

2 Scald the orange with boiling water and peel the skin finely. Cut the butter into small chunks, add the sugar and mix for one minute, until the mixture is fluffy.

3 Add the 2 eggs, vanilla and ½ teaspoon of orange peel. Continue mixing.

4 Add the flour into the mixing bowl and combine all the ingredients with a spatula, then shape into a ball, cover with plastic wrap and set in the fridge for at least an hour.

5 Heat the oven to 180°C. Roll the dough until it is only 3 mm thick and then start cutting out circles with a diameter of about 6–7 cm. Beat the remaining egg and glaze each circle with the mixture to make sure the biscuits stay intact as they bake.

6 In the centre of each biscuit, place ½ teaspoon of filling. Fold three sides over to create the form of a three-sided pocket (as shown above) and arrange on a baking sheet covered with wax paper. Bake for 25 minutes until they are golden.

7 Allow the biscuits to cool before serving as the filling can be quite hot.

Eitan is an expert at folding the edges of his hamantashen.

HUMMUS

Chickpea spread
Soak chickpeas: 12 hours
Cook: ⏱ 40 minutes
Prep time: ⏱ 10 minutes

½ cup dried chickpeas (130 g)

½ tsp baking soda

6 cups water (1½ l)

⅓ cup tahini (85 ml)

1 garlic clove

2 tbsp lemon

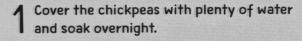
½ cup water (125 ml)

½ tbsp salt

1 Cover the chickpeas with plenty of water and soak overnight.

2 Drain the chickpeas. Add 6 cups of water, and the baking soda and cook on a low heat for 40 minutes, until the chickpeas are soft.

3 Use a blender to mix the cooked chickpeas with the other ingredients until you have a smooth paste. If it is too thick, add a bit of water. Serve with olive oil and sprinkle with za'atar*.

* Za'atar is a Middle Eastern blend of spices, sumac and sesame.

Ayala likes to have a bowl of hummus for breakfast.

POCKETFUL OF POPPYSEED

▸ The Jewish holiday **Purim** celebrates the defeat of Haman, a court official who sentenced the Jewish people to death.
▸ During Purim, there are energetic parties. One of the most popular Purim treats is **hamantashen***, which means 'Haman's pockets' (these treats are also called Haman's 'hat' or 'ears').

* See the recipe on the previous page.

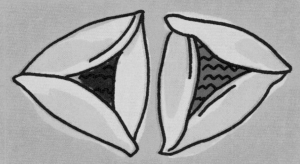

WORKING HARD TO RELAX

▸ At the end of a work week, even God has to take a break. That period of rest and relaxation is known as the **Shabbat** (or the Sabbath), which begins every Friday evening and lasts just over 24 hours. Any type of activity related to labour is forbidden. Even cooking is not allowed.
▸ This means that meals have to be prepared in advance. One popular shabbat dish is called **cholent**. It is slow cooked for a long time, so it's ready for Saturday lunchtime.

PRECIOUS OIL

▸ 2,000 years ago, Judah Maccabee helped the Jewish people regain control of the Second Temple in Jerusalem. He then led efforts to purge the temple of Greek and Roman influences.
▸ Olive oil was needed for this sacred ritual. While there was only enough oil for a single day, miraculously the flame kept burning for eight days!
▸ The holiday of **Hanukkah** commemorates this amazing event. Candles are burned in a special candelabrum called a *menorah* and deep-fried treats, both sweet and savoury, are enjoyed.

LATKES
Potato pancakes

SUFGANIYOT
Jam-filled donuts

SWEET NEW YEAR

▸ **Rosh Hashanah** is the Jewish new year celebration. This holiday also commemorates the divine creation of the world and the first humans, Adam and Eve.
▸ The theme of this holiday is sweetness and good fortune: apples dipped in honey, dates, pomegranate a sweet carrot stew known as Tzimmes and loaves o **Challah** bread speckled with raisins are all enjoyed.

THE FIG MYSTERY

- Humans many have been cultivating figs ❽ for thousands of years, but it took quite a bit of time to fully understand the fruit's unpredictable life cycle.
- An individual fig is made up of over 1,000 tiny flowers that come from over 1,000 tiny seeds.

- As in the case of other seed-bearing plants, the female flowers need to be pollinated with grains from the male flowers. Since male and female fig flowers develop at different times, the grains of pollen from male flowers have to be transported from another flower.

- This is achieved by a small insect known as a fig wasp. It deposits its eggs inside the fig, but ends up trapped inside! When the fig blooms, the wasp's offspring hatch and escape. The females spread the fig pollen to the other figs that they crawl through to lay their own eggs.

BEAN BABIES

- Humans have been feasting on legumes for thousands of years. Popular beans include green beans, soy, peas, broad beans, lentils, peanuts and tamarind seeds.

- **Chickpeas** are also legumes and are the main ingredient in **hummus** ㉗ as well as **falafel** ㉙* (which originally comes from Egypt).

  * Find out more about Egyptian falafels on page 98.

SMALL BUT POWERFUL

- They might be tiny, but **sesame seeds** are packed with healthy fats. They can be consumed whole, as an oil or as a paste known as tahini.
- **Tahini** is a base ingredient for many recipes, including sauces, baked goods and ice cream.
- It's impossible to talk about tahini without mentioning sesame halva*. A proper hummus also requires a dollop of tahini.

  * See more about halva on page 7.

WORK, HUMMUS, COMMUNITY

- More than a century ago, the first settlers arrive in what later became the official state of Israel. They began setting up cooperative farming communities known as a **kibbutz**.
- The members of a kibbutz, no matter who they are, all share the same rights and duties.
- There wasn't time to prepare elaborate dishes at a kibbutz, so workers would enjoy a hearty breakfast of vegetables, cheese, eggs, olives, hummus, bread, coffee and fresh juices. Today, this is known as an **Israeli breakfast**.

CHINA
PEARLS OF HISTORY

SHANG DYNASTY
1600–1046 BCE

XIA DYNASTY
c.2070–c.1600 BCE

ZHOU DYNASTY
1046–256 BCE

QIN DYNASTY
221–207 BCE

Yu the Great

Wu Ding

Wu Wang

Qin Shi Huang

▸ China is among the most ancient empires in the world. Its culinary discoveries have reached the furthest corners of the globe.

▸ For thousands of years, each region of this vast country developed their own individual customs and cuisines. Their unique histories, climate, agriculture and ingredients all contributed to Chinese cuisine.

▸ Tea, chopsticks and a penchant for soy are all elements shared by these regional kitchens. While rice is a staple for many Chinese kitchens, wheat noodles and buns are more popular in the north.

▸ Despite these cuisines being incredibly varied, there are links that unite them together if you look close enough. While it isn't useful to consider common ingredients, it is useful to look at shared ideas. For example, the Chinese approach to culinary arts is to prepare each dish meticulously and with great care. Universal to all Chinese households is the love of feasting and socialising.

BEAN OF ALL TRADES

▸ Together with wheat, corn and rice, **soy** makes up one of the fundamental foodstuffs consumed by both people and domesticated animals. Thanks to the exceptionally high levels of protein soy contains, it is a strong contender to replace meat products. This is especially relevant today, when raising animals is becoming costly both in terms of the financial and environmental impact.

▸ Soybeans grow in pods, like peas, but unlike peas, they remain quite hard, flavourless and generally inedible even after they are cooked. In Chinese kitchens, as well as in other places across Southeast Asia, there are multiple ways to process soy to create many tasty specialities.

SIPS OF ENLIGHTENMENT

▸ **Tea** was discovered in China between 4,000–5,000 years ago. By the time of the Tang Dynasty, it was the preferred drink for most Chinese people.

▸ During this period, the sage **Lu Yu** described the method for brewing the ideal cup of tea, from selecting the leaves to preparing the water.

▸ According to the master, drinking tea was a restorative ritual for the body and the spirit as it helps achieve a sense of inner harmony.

SOY MILK

TOFU

SOY SAUCE

TEMPEH
A block of fermented soy that originated in Indonesia (see more on page 32).

MISO
A Japanese paste made of fermented soy that is used as a condiment.

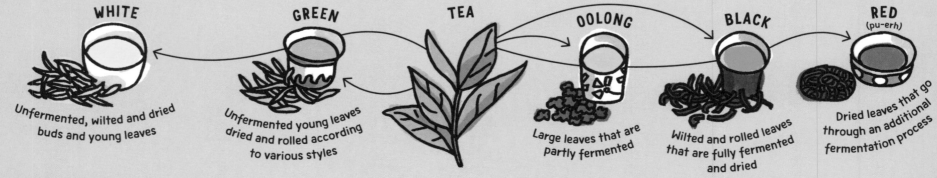

WHITE
Unfermented, wilted and dried buds and young leaves

GREEN
Unfermented young leaves dried and rolled according to various styles

TEA

OOLONG
Large leaves that are partly fermented

BLACK
Wilted and rolled leaves that are fully fermented and dried

RED (pu-erh)
Dried leaves that go through an additional fermentation process

FIVE IN ONE

▸ While there are countless varieties of tea in the world, they all come from a single type of plant: the eternally green *Camellia sinensis*. The differences in colour, flavour and aroma all depend on how the leaves are prepared after they are picked.

FRIENDLY FERMENTATION

▸ In China, the full spectrum of soy products is referred to as **dou fu** (similar to its Japanese equivalent 'tofu').

▸ Tofu is similar in texture to cottage cheese, but it can change depending on structure, hardness, colour and aroma. Tofu can be smooth and delicate, but it can also be fibrous or spongy.

▸ The more delicate varieties go perfectly with a range of dishes, as tofu tends to absorb ingredients and seasonings.

1 Gather the harvest.

2 Separate the seeds from the pod.

3 Soak the seeds.

4 Grind.

5 Boil.

6 Separate the soy milk.

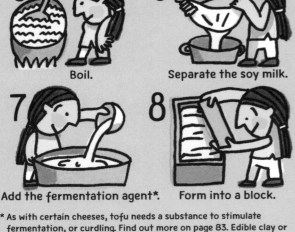

7 Add the fermentation agent*.

8 Form into a block.

* As with certain cheeses, tofu needs a substance to stimulate fermentation, or curdling. Find out more on page 83. Edible clay or seawater is used to ferment tofu.

MAPO TOFU

Tofu in a spicy sauce

🕐 30 minutes, 3×🍜

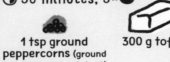 1 tsp ground peppercorns (ground Szechuan pepper is best)

 300 g tofu

 4 tbsp tomato paste

 1½ tsp gochugaru powder (or cayenne)

3 garlic cloves

 2 cm strip of ginger

⅓ cup cooking oil (85 ml) (peanut or sesame is best)

 250 g ground beef

 1⅕ cups water (300 ml)

2 tbsp soy sauce

1 tbsp starch (e.g. potato flour)

 bunch of spring onions

salt

🌶 Mapo doufu is supposed to be very spicy, so feel free to add as much and as many spicy ingredients as you like.

🍚 In China, this dish is prepared on a base made of fermented broad beans and soy, but it's hard to find elsewhere, so we've left it out of this recipe.

1 Bring the water to the boil in a small pot with a teaspoon of salt. Add the tofu and cook for 1–2 minutes on low heat. Remove the tofu and when it cools down, cut into small chunks.

2 Mix the tomato paste with the gochugaru powder. Chop the garlic and ginger and set aside.

3 Heat the oil in a large pan. When hot, add the meat. Season with salt and cook for a few minutes, then add the spicy tomato paste, pepper, garlic and ginger. Cook for five more minutes.

4 Add the water from the pot and soy sauce. Add the tofu and mix gently. Cook the mixture for several minutes.

5 Finally, add a spoonful of starch (dissolved in a spoonful of water). Serve with rice and garnish with chopped spring onions.

Wang Wei prefers her mapo doufu extra spicy. The hotter, the better!

FIVE DYNASTIES AND TEN KINGDOMS
907—960

WESTERN XIA
1038—1227

Li Yuanhao

SONG DYNASTY
960—1279

YUAN DYNASTY
1271—1368

Kublai Khan

LIAO DYNASTY
916—1125

Taizu

JIN DYNASTY
1115—1234

Taizu of Jin

Taizu of Song

STARCHY STAR

▶ It's almost impossible to imagine the world without **rice** — it could even be claimed that it's the most important agricultural product in human history!

▶ Comparing rice with other starchy foods*, it's easy to see its advantages. Rice can be dried, so can be stored for a long time without going bad, and rice harvests are more abundant than those of other grains. In addition, rice doesn't require much processing.

* Read more about starchy foods on page 102.

LONG-GRAIN RICE

SHORT-GRAIN RICE

CONGEE (also zhou or jook)

Rice porridge

 2 hours, 4×

½ cup rice (90 g)

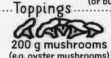 3 cups water (750 ml) (or bullion)

Toppings

boiled chicken (optional)

200 g mushrooms (e.g. oyster mushrooms)

soy sauce

1 tsp ginger powder

fresh coriander

marinated vegetables

spring onions

peanuts

chopped salad

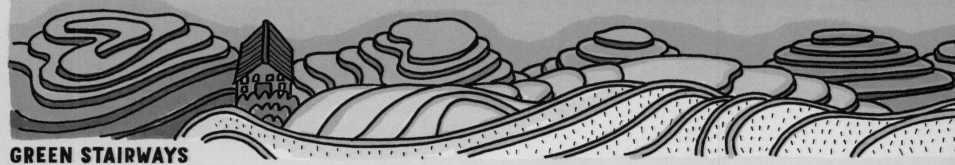

GREEN STAIRWAYS

▶ There are about 8,000 varieties of rice cultivated today, feeding about half of humanity! Rice is often grown in regions that experience lots of rain — some crops are even submerged in several metres of water. There are also 'dry' fields of rice. In China, traditional **rice terraces** produce a lot of rice — they are both picturesque and labour-intensive.

▶ These lovely structures make it possible to grow rice even on hilltops! The terraces are so hydrated, it is possible for them to have up to three harvests a year.

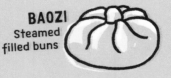
BAOZI
Steamed filled buns

YUAN XIAO
Sticky rice balls with a sweet filling

SHA HE FEN
Wide rice noodle

FEN SI
Starch-based 'glass' noodles

MI FEN
Thin rice noodles

MANTOU
Steamed buns (no filling)

WONTON
Dumplings filled with meat or shrimp, often served in a broth

JIAOZI
Crescent-shaped filled dumplings

MIAN
Hand-pulled noodles of varying lengths

ARRAY OF NOODLES

▶ When you think of noodles, it's probably Italian cuisine that comes to mind.

But China actually has the greatest array of doughy goodies — their noodles, dumplings and buns are made using different types of flour.

MING DYNASTY
1368—1644

QING DYNASTY
1644—1911

Qianlong

Hongwu

Congee is best known as a breakfast dish. While it may seem similar to porridge, it's actually a savoury dish served with toppings such as coriander, chives, garlic or ginger.

1 Rinse the rice in cold water several times. Add three cups of water, bring to boil and cook for 2 hours on a very low heat, stirring from time to time. Add the chicken (if using).

2 Cut the mushrooms into strips and mix with the soy sauce and ginger. Set aside for 30 minutes.

3 Heat the oil in a pan, add the marinated mushrooms (drained) and fry them on a high heat. Then drain on a paper towel.

4 Serve the congee in bowls alongside the toppings.

Li Min starts each day with a hearty bowl of congee with plenty of toppings.

---

4 Rice comes to Europe

1 Rice was first farmed here

5 Rice comes to the Americas

3 Rice comes to Africa

2 Rice comes to India

SHOOTING STARS

▶ **Bamboo** is a type of plant that could have come straight out of a science fiction novel. It can grow at a speed of nearly one metre per day — reaching up to 30 metres in total. It is so strong that bamboo is used to make houses, bridges and other durable constructions. Most of these shoots bloom only once every dozen or so years. What's more, all the plants in a single group — making up entire forests — bloom all at once and then die, leaving behind a sea of seeds. The strangest thing about bamboo is that no one really knows how or why this happens!

▶ If that wasn't enough, bamboo shoots can also be quite a tasty snack. It's enough to peel its skin as soon as it is out of the ground, and then boil away the bitterness.

AROUND THE WORLD

▶ World experts still haven't agreed on when and where the first rice fields might have been cultivated. It's most likely that rice was first farmed in a region between eastern India and south China about 12,000 years ago.

▶ Over the course of a thousand years, rice gradually spread throughout the world, and ended its journey in the Americas.

JAPAN
HEALTHY AND HEARTY

- Japanese delicacies are famous across the globe: broths full of umami flavours, fine slices of sashimi and, of course, sushi.
- The people of the many islands that make up Japan were traditionally thought to be wary of adopting any new cuisine from the continent. They preferred instead to focus on local ingredients. The rich flavours and combinations of Japanese cuisine are therefore due to the ingenuity of Japanese chefs and the fact they made the most of just a few essential ingredients.
- When Japan opened itself up to influences from the rest of the world in the modern era, waves of culinary influence flowed in. Rice, soy, wheat and tea made their way to Japan from China. Even milk and potatoes became popular due to improved relations with the United States over a century ago.
- The one element that has shaped Japanese culinary arts through the centuries is the desire for beauty. Even snacks and appetizers are prepared with as much care as a ceremonial meal. Japanese cuisine is always a feast for the eyes and the palate.

SEA GREENS

- Japanese people traditionally follow a plant-based diet because of their religious beliefs and also because Japan's hilly islands just don't have enough room for animals to roam. **Seaweed** is among the most popular greens in Japanese cuisine.
- Billions of leaves of seaweed are still consumed each year, either fresh or dried. Seaweed has a unique savoury flavour and rich mineral content. It can also be used as a thickening agent.

NORI
Available in the form of thin sheets that are produced using the same traditional method as Japanese paper

KOMBU
Its large leaves are either dried or marinated just after gathering

WAKAME
Eaten fresh, dried or in powdered form as a topping or additive

TURBOPOWERED GREENS

- In 1908, the Japanese chemist and scholar Kikunae Ikeda discovered that kombu seaweed is packed with a type of amino acid that is essential to Japanese cuisine. After a series of tests, it was found that glutamic acid is responsible for the 'meaty' flavour of even meat-free dishes. Professor Ikeda coined the term 'umami' to describe this flavour, which literally translates as 'delicious'.
- In the years that followed, Ikeda's colleagues would go on to discover other sources of umami, including bonito flakes and shiitake mushrooms.

Kikunae Ikeda

Shintaro Kodama

Akira Kuninaka

MYSTERIOUS DISAPPEARANCES

▶ Up until very recently, the cultivation of nori ⑥ was a highly unpredictable undertaking. The underwater fields often contained no new plants, giving nori the nickname of 'lucky' or 'gambler's grass'.

▶ The mystery was solved by **Dr Kathleen Drew-Baker**, who discovered that nori seeds typically become attached to cracks in the shells of molluscs. When the water gets too cold, the sea creatures drift away and take the seeds with them.

▶ Dr Drew suggested that seaweed growers set up nets full of eggshells, and this has greatly increased nori production.

Dr Drew-Baker

1. Boil the rice.
2. Add koji mushrooms.
3. Boil the soy.
4. Grind the soy.
5. Mix the soy and rice with salt.
6. Allow fermentation to begin.

INTENSELY UMAMI

▶ **Miso** is a thick, savoury paste that is made when soy is fermented (it can also be made from rice or other grains). It is used in miso soup and many other dishes where a dash of umami is desired.

FORBIDDEN FOODS

▶ When Buddhism became one of Japan's main religions over 1,400 years ago, meat consumption began to be considered at odds with its beliefs. For instance, Buddhism forbids the taking of a life and many scholars related this rule not only to the world of humans, but also animals (seafood and fish were not typically considered as meat).

▶ Today, these dietary restrictions don't have as much influence in Japan, but the main staples of the national diet are still fish and vegetables.

MISO SOUP

Umami-flavoured soup ⏱ 15 minutes, 4×🍚

3 tbsp dried wakame

½ cup cold water (125 ml)

6 cups water (1½ l)

2 tsp dashi* bullion powder

3 tbsp miso paste (60 g)

1 tofu cube (200 g)

1 bunch of chives

1 handful of fresh mung beans (optional)

* Dashi is a broth made of kombu seaweed and flakes of katsuobushi (see more on the next page).

Haru likes to have a nice cup of miso at the end of every meal.

1. Soak the wakame in ½ cup of cold water and set aside for 10 minutes.

2. In the meantime, bring 6 cups of water to the boil and add the dashi and miso. Mix well and let the mixture come back to boiling.

3. Cut the tofu into smaller cubes. Dice the chives on an angle. Add both to the broth and cook for 5 minutes.

4. Drain the wakame and cut into thick pieces, add to the broth together with the mung beans (if using) and cook for another minute or so.

SALTY FISH

¹ More on fish preservation methods on page 57. ² See more on page 65.

▶ Limited access to meat and religious restrictions led many Japanese to shun beef and pork in favour of seafood. Before the time of refrigerators, it was quite a challenge to transport fresh fish inland.

▶ This is why various methods of preserving fish[1] became popular. In Japan, it is referred to as **narezushi**, which simply means 'salted fish'.

▶ Delicate slices of fish are interlaid with rice (which is then discarded when it is time to consume the fish). Over time, the lactic acid[2] in the rice pickles the fish. This precursor to sushi was for a long time the centrepiece of most meals.

▶ Today, vinegar is used to ferment the rice and the fish is served raw. This relatively novel method for preparing sushi only came about some 300 years ago.

> Hey! I was saving that for later!

> Oh, sorry!

TINY BITES

▶ **Sushi** is the most widely recognised of all Japanese foods. It's served as both a delicacy in high-end restaurants, as well as at fast-food chains* and local takeaway counters.

* Read more about fast food on page 37.

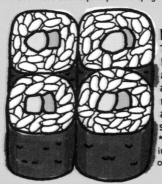

MAKIZUSHI 8

These 'sushi rolls' are made by placing a layer of rice and selected ingredients across a sheet of roasted nori seaweed, rolling it up and then cutting the roll into smaller discs.

* Some makizushi also use different ingredients for the outer layer instead of nori.

OSHIZUSHI 9

Also known as 'pressed sushi', a block of rice is compressed inside a special wooden box 11 with selected ingredients (cooked or fermented). The block is cut into smaller pieces before serving.

▶ Of course, the quality of the sushi served varies across this range of establishments. Mastering the preparation of sushi is a skill that requires a great deal of knowledge, focus and years of practice.

NIGIRIZUSHI 3 10

This type of sushi is prepared on a single layer of rice that is formed by hand and topped with a slice of fish or seafood.

CHIRASHIZUSHI 4 12

Also known as 'scattered sushi', the toppings are served on top of a bed of rice in a bowl.

Sushi is typically served with slices of pickled ginger (gari), soy sauce (which provides a kick of umami flavour), eye-watering wasabi, white radish (daikon) and green tea.

ONIGIRI

Tasty rice balls
Rice preparation: ⏱ 1 hour
Formation: ⏱ 20 minutes, 12–14×🍙

 2 cups sushi rice (400 g)

 2¾ cups water (690 ml)

 2 sheets nori

·······Stuffing·······

 ½ can tuna in brine (60 g)

1 tsp soy sauce

30 g smoked or baked salmon

 a few umeboshi (or other pickled fruits)

 salt

 sesame for garnish

Traditionally, onigiri 5 is a rice ball filled with a sweet-and-sour filling made of **umeboshi** (a pickled apricot-like fruit) or flakes of bonito that have been dried and fermented (**katsuobushi**). You can also make onigiri with any filling of your choice (e.g. pickled pumpkin, or pear, shrimp, anchovies) or no filling at all.

1 Pour the rice into a bowl and fill with a generous amount of water. Mix the grains around in the bowl then drain the water. Repeat until the water runs clear.

2 Drain the rice and place in a pot with the water. Set aside to soak for at least 30 minutes (up to a maximum of 8 hours). Cut the nori into strips that are around 7 x 3cm.

3 Set the rice to boil and then reduce the heat to low, cover the pot and boil for 15 minutes without stirring. Set the covered pot aside for 10–15 minutes.

4 Gently stir the rice and let it cool. Onigiri is easiest to form when the rice is warm.

ESSENTIAL SOY

▶ Alongside miso, one of the most popular ingredients for umami flavour is **soy sauce❶**. This salty sauce was first prepared in China during the time of the Zhou Dynasty*.

▶ The many varieties of soy sauce come about when soybeans and wheat are fermented. In Japan and China, soy sauce is used to flavour dishes in the same way as Europeans use salt.

* Find out more about soy and the history of China on page 16.

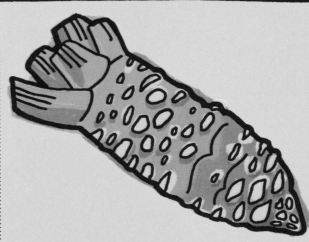

PERFECTION

▶ Japanese tradition states that the most important part of preparing fish is to keep its unique flavour and texture. The processes of cooking, frying, baking or fermenting can often change the original flavour of the fish quite dramatically.

▶ This is likely to be the reason why the most popular food in Japanese bars and restaurants is **sashimi❼**, which is essentially slices of raw fish, squid or other seafood.

EYE-WATERING WASABI

▶ **Wasabi❷** often accompanies Japanese dishes, served as a small portion of very fine shavings. Its sharp flavour rises all the way up into the nostrils.

▶ Outside of Japan, it is difficult to get hold of fresh wasabi roots. It is often suplemented with a paste or powder.

▶ Instead of wasabi, some European restaurants serve grated horseradish* — which is coloured green. Even though the two roots are very different, the same peculiar effect on the nose is achieved!

* See more about horseradish on page 71.

5 Drain the tuna and mix with soy sauce. Flake the salmon. Mince the umeboshi (or alternative pickles).

6 Wet your hands and sprinkle your fingers with a little bit of salt. Place 2–3 teaspoons of salt into your hand and squeeze tightly, making a triangle shape. Make a small indent in the middle for your filling, then seal it back up by squeezing the ball with your hand again.

7 Place a strip of nori underneath the ongiri and sprinkle with sesame.

Onigiri can be served in a variety of ways.

Yuman packs onigiri for her son's lunch each day.

INDIA
DIVINE DAIRY AND SACRED SPICES

INDUS VALLEY CIVILISATION

▶ As far back as 5,000 years ago, an advanced civilisation formed in the Indus Valley (modern-day India). Its lengthy history and multitude of customs, languages and religions influenced the many cuisines of India.

There is no single Indian culinary tradition — every region has its own signature style of cooking.

▶ Indian food is very much shaped by faith and tradition. Holy Hindu scriptures say that what we eat not only impacts our body, but our spirit too. The scriptures also advised how to prepare food.

▶ Because of these religious beliefs, many Hindus don't eat meat (beef, in particular).

▶ The idea behind this comes from the concept of ahimsa, the principle of non-violence that

HOLY COW

▶ In India, cows are endowed with a respect that dates back 4,000 years ❸. They are considered sacred and are free to roam the streets. The reason is certainly rooted in religion, but there are also some practical factors to consider...

▶ Milking cows provides a great deal more food than if they were raised for their meat: cream, yoghurt, ice cream, different types of cheese, butter and ghee ❺. Cattle are also helpful farmhands, helping to pull ploughs and other equipment. Cow manure is also a great fertiliser and can be used as fuel for stoves. Cows don't need much upkeep but they give a great deal in return!

▶ Even the Indian government has made significant efforts to protect cows, forbidding their slaughter.

KRISHNA

One of the most popular and revered Hindu gods of compassion and love, often depicted as a holy shepherd of cattle.

MILK BARFI (also burfi, borfi)
Creamy snack bars

🕙 10 minutes prep, chill overnight, 14 ×

6 tbsp ghee or butter (80 g)

½ cup milk (125 mL)

1 cup powdered sugar (120 g)

2 cups powdered milk (140 g)

¼ tsp ground cardamom

Burfi is the first treat Rahul learned to make.

1 Melt the ghee or butter in a pan over low heat, then add the milk, sugar and powdered milk. Stir vigorously as you continue to heat the mixture, until it thickens.

2 Add the cardamom and stir it all the way through the mixture.

3 Place the mixture on a greased plate or pan, creating a layer at least 2 cm thick. Put into the fridge to cool overnight, then cut into bars. Store in a cool place.

states all living beings are part of a universal whole. The belief in reincarnation is also part of ahimsa.

► Curries are among the most well-known Indian specialties, typically made with spices, and a sauce made of coconut, tomato or yoghurt.

There are also lots of different types of biryani — rice served with vegetables, meat, and a hearty amount of seasoning ⑥.

► Dishes are often served with a flatbread known as chapati ④ or naan, baked in a clay tandoori oven.

► In India, it is customary to eat with the right hand, as the left hand is considered 'unclean'. Indian cuisine is ideal for people who adore fragrant spices, sweet treats and creative vegetarian dishes.

Hindu faith guarantees the protection over all animals, however, cows hold a special place in religious writings and depictions.

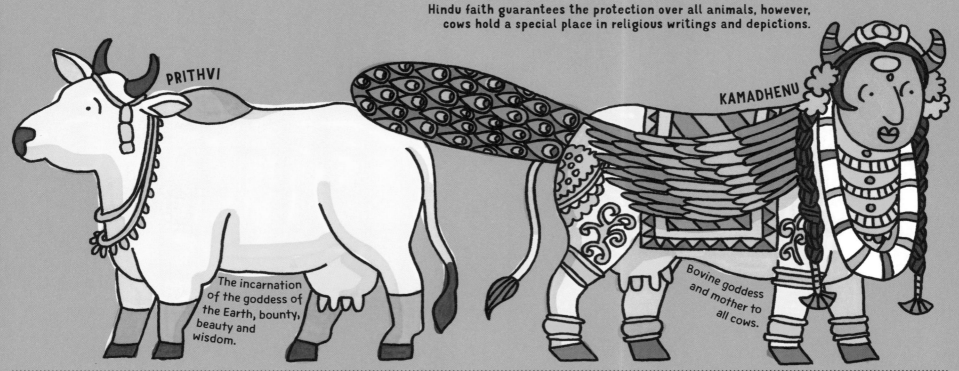

PRITHVI
The incarnation of the goddess of the Earth, bounty, beauty and wisdom.

KAMADHENU
Bovine goddess and mother to all cows.

STAYING FRESH

► Ghee ⑤ is a type of clarified butter* that is entirely made up of fat. Even when ghee is stored at room temperature, it stays fresh. For this reason it predates the invention of refrigeration by thousands of years.

► Ghee is considered an ideal product because it is produced from pure cow's milk. In India, it is used for nearly everything: preparing curries and sweets, frying up spices, and as a spread.

► Ghee is also offered as a sacred gift to the gods and it is believed to have certain health benefits.

* See more on page 105.

1 Heat the milk.

2 Skim the cream that rises to the top.

3 Add a bit of yoghurt to the cream.

4 Churn the butter.

5 Separate the butter from the rest of the mass (this is the buttermilk).

6 Heat the butter.

7 Skim the foam off the top (the last bits of milk rising to the surface).

8 Your ghee is ready!

ALL TYPES OF HERBS ARE CULTIVATED IN INDIA

SPECTACULAR SPICES

► Indian cuisine is best known for its hot and fragrant spice combinations. This type of spice mix is known as a **masala**❶[1], while dishes cooked in a spicy sauce are known as curries, even when there is no **curry** leaf or powder in the dish at all.

[1] The first masalas were mainly composed of turmeric powder, ginger and garlic. The first people to inhabit the Indus Valley used this mixture in their cooking as far back as 4,000 years ago.

► One of the most famous mixes is **garam masala**[2] made up of cumin, black pepper, coriander seeds, cardamom, cloves, cinnamon and nutmeg.

[2] Garam masala is an essential seasoning in the preparation of rajma chawal (or rajma masala) — see the recipe at the bottom of this page.

ASAFETIDA❼
also known as 'stinking gum'
Sap is extracted from the stem and roots and dried. This spice is best known for its pungent smell, which disappears when it is cooked, leaving behind a rich oniony-leek flavour.

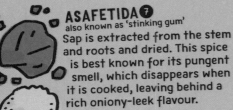

FENUGREEK⓫
seeds   leaves
This herb has a tangy smell and bitter flavour.

PEPPER⓭
As the fruit of the flowering vine known as *Piper nigrum*, black peppercorns are what we get when the fruits are cooked and dried.
White pepper is the same peppercorns but with the dark outside layer removed.
Green pepper is made up of dried unripe peppercorns.

green   black
CARDAMOM❽
These are the dried seeds of the cardamom plant. Once they are ground, the seeds quickly lose their aroma, which is why they are typically used in cooking just after grinding.

CLOVES⓬
The dried buds of the tree known by the Latin name *Syzygium aromaticum*, which is native to Indonesia. Cloves have an intense, sharp flavour and vibrant scent.
Fresh buds

NUTMEG
dried seed

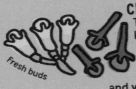

Both of these spices come from the nutmeg tree and share a similar flavour, however mace is a bit subtler.

MACE (NUTMEG FLOWER)
dried seed coating

CINNAMON❾
Cinnamon verum is the dried bark of the Ceylon cinnamon tree, which is native to Sri Lanka. Known as 'true cinnamon', it is considered superior to its more affordable alternative, 'cassia cinnamon'.
Ceylon   Cassia

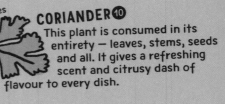

seeds   leaves
CORIANDER❿
This plant is consumed in its entirety – leaves, stems, seeds and all. It gives a refreshing scent and citrusy dash of flavour to every dish.

TURMERIC❷⓰
Boiled, dried and ground into a powder, these roots have a gently piquant flavour that is related to ginger. It has been used as a spice for thousands of years and its golden colour has also been used as a dye.

RAJMA CHAWAL
Spicy beans and rice
Soaking time (beans): 8 hours
Cooking time: 60–90 minutes
Preparation: 45 minutes, 3×

 1 cup dried red kidney beans (175 g)
 4 cups cold water (1 l)
salt
 1 large onion
 ginger stem (3 cm)
3 garlic cloves
1 can chopped tomatoes (400 g)

5 tbsp vegetable oil (75 ml)
¼ tsp chilli powder (or cayenne pepper)
1 tbsp clarified butter (ghee)

2 laurel leaves
1 tsp garam masala
a bunch of fresh coriander

½ tbsp ground cumin
1 tsp dried fenugreek leaves (optional)
boiled rice for serving

1 Cover the beans with water and soak for at least 8 hours. Drain the beans, rinse with fresh water and cook in a covered pot on a low heat for 60–90 minutes. The beans should be soft to the touch but not mushy. Towards the end, add a teaspoon of salt. Drain the beans, keeping the water in a separate container for later.

2 Dice the onion, peel the ginger and garlic cloves. Mix them in a blender with two tablespoons of water and set aside. Blend the tomatoes into a paste.

CANDY CANES

► People have always been suckers for the sweet taste of fruit and honey. Today, sugar is the most popular sweetener, but it is nonetheless a relatively recent invention.

► As far back as 10,000 years ago, sugar cane 15, began to be cultivated in Asia. The sweet cane juice was squeezed out of its stalks. It wasn't until 8,000 years later that Indian farmers came upon the idea of drying this juice out in the sun. In this way, they obtained granules that were essentially the first type of sugar. These granules were used to sweeten drinks and dishes.

► After originating in India, **sugar** made its way across the world. For centuries, it was considered a luxury. Today, sugar is so accessible that most humans consume too much of it. People still press cane juice today, but sugar can also be obtained from sugar beets* through a method perfected 150 years ago.

* More on page 71.

1
The stalks are cut into strips.

2
The strips are put through a press.

3
The sugar cane juice is boiled. The water evaporates and a syrup known as molasses is left behind.

4
Microscopic grains of sugar are added to stimulate the production of more crystals.

5
The crystals are separated from the rest of the mixture.

6
The brown sugar is now ready to enjoy (or it is bleached to make white sugar).

Because both sugar and lemons are native to India, it's widely believed that the first lemonade came from there too. The traditional version contains lemon juice, lime juice and ginger, along with the addition of mint, apples, pomegranate seeds, cumin or saffron.

3 Heat the oil, adding the laurel leaves. Cook for a minute, stirring the whole time.

4 Add the diced onion and cook for 4 minutes on medium heat, until soft. Add the ginger and garlic blend and cook for another minute.

5 Increase the heat and add the tomato paste. Add salt to taste and cook for 8 minutes, stirring from time to time until the mixture thickens.

Priya makes rajma chawal every week.

6 Add the cumin, chilli and half a teaspoon of garam masala (save the other half for later).

7 Add the beans, along with 2 cups of the bean water. Cook under a lid for 15 minutes on low heat, then increase the heat, remove the lid and cook for another 10–15 minutes. Add the remaining garam masala, along with the fenugreek leaves (if desired) and a tablespoon of clarified butter. You can also mash up some of the beans to thicken the mixture.

8 Serve with rice and garnish with fresh coriander.

VIETNAM
FRESH AND FISHY

▶ The history of Vietnam starts with the glorious legacies of the Văn Lang and Âu Lạc kingdoms. The latter was eventually conquered by the Chinese 2,200 years ago and the north of Vietnam remained under Chinese rule for the next 1,000 years.

▶ The wealth that the Chinese brought to Vietnam had a great influence on the local cuisine, introducing dishes such as dumplings and customs such as eating with chopsticks.

▶ There were also influences from Europe. Vietnamese ingredients packed in to make the famous bánh mì ❻ is just one result of French colonialism. Many herbs and spices ❽ now essential to Vietnamese cuisine originally came from India via historic trade routes.

▶ The Vietnamese cuisine does not in any way lack originality, however. Using salad leaves and herbs ❾ as a wrap is a local invention. And any new ideas from afar have always been adapted to local preferences, creating a unique culinary experience.

1

Fishermen bring in the catch of the day.

2

Anchovies are stored in a barrel.

3

Salt is added.

4

The fish is left to ferment for a whole year.

5

The sauce is filtered and bottled.

SPLENDIDLY PUNGENT

▶ One of the most important ingredients in many Vietnamese dishes is a distinctive **fish sauce** ❺ typically made from salted and fermented anchovies called Nước chấm. It is a universal condiment that is used to season dishes, much like soy sauce* is used in Japan and China.

* See more on page 23.

BÁNH XÈO
Crispy stuffed crêpes
⏱ 45 minutes, 6× 🌮

Crêpe batter

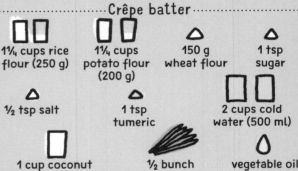

1¼ cups rice flour (250 g)	1¼ cups potato flour (200 g)	150 g wheat flour	1 tsp sugar
½ tsp salt	1 tsp tumeric		2 cups cold water (500 ml)
1 cup coconut milk (250 ml)	½ bunch of chives		vegetable oil for frying

Toppings

300 g bacon	200–300 g fresh or frozen shrimp	1 large onion
4 handfuls of mung bean sprouts	1 head of butter lettuce	2 short green cucumbers
2 small carrots	a handful of fresh coriander and mint	salt

Nước mắm pha dipping sauce

2 cloves garlic	1 chilli pepper	juice ½ a lime
¼ cup sugar (55 g)	6 tbsp fish sauce	½ cup warm water (125 ml)

1 Combine all the different types of flour with the sugar, salt and turmeric in a bowl. Add the cold water and coconut milk and whisk. Chop the chives and add to the mix. Cover and set aside for 30 minutes.

2 Cut the bacon into slices around ½ cm thick. Salt the bacon and shrimp. Cut the onion into thick strips. Wash and dry the lettuce. Peel the

cucumbers and carrots and use the peeler to make thin strips (like ribbons).

3 Chop the garlic and chilli, then add the rest of the dipping sauce ingredients.

4 Heat 2 tablespoons of oil until it is very hot. Place 4 strips of bacon and 2–3 shrimps in the pan. Fry on high for 5 minutes, flipping from time to time. Add a few slivers of onion and fry for another 2–3 minutes.

5 Make sure none of the ingredients have stuck to the bottom of the pan. Add another tablespoon of oil and pour in a generous portion of batter. Spread it across the bottom of the pan. Fry your crêpe for 3 minutes, then lower the heat and cover the pan for a few minutes.

6 Sprinkle the bean sprouts over half the crêpe and fold in half. Cover again and fry for a moment longer.

7 This is a meal that you are meant to eat with your hands. Cut a piece of crêpe and place it in one of the lettuce leaves. Add cucumber and carrot, along with a dash of herbs. Fold up, dip in the sauce and enjoy!

Duc prefers extra shrimp in his bánh xèo.

BOWLFUL OF GOODNESS

▶ **Phở** soup ❶ is popular around the world. There are countless versions of this hearty soup, but all of them are based on a bone broth flavoured with onion, ginger and other seasonings. Every bowl comes with an array of fresh toppings to choose from: rice noodles, strips of meat, fresh herbs, sprouts, vegetables, fish sauce and other condiments ❹.

Steaming hot pot | Fresh toppings | Travelling kitchen **gánh phở**

▶ A number of researchers have suggested that phở came about as product of the French love of beef. When Vietnam was under French occupation, the country began to raise more cattle and consume more beef. The beef bones and leftovers were eventually adapted into an early version of what we know as phở soup today.

Travelling soup kitchens are a local tradition. Sellers serve steaming bowls of soup and ingredients from pots they carry on a pole across their shoulders.

1, 2, 3, GO!

▶ Vietnamese dishes are typically full of wonderfully fresh ingredients that are either served cold or quickly fried up in a **wok**.

▶ This method of cooking is called a **stir fry** ❼. It is not only fast, but the quick cooking time helps retain the colour, flavour and texture of the ingredients ❸.

A wok is a deep round-bottomed frying pan that originated in China.

SPRING IS IN

▶ Another one of Vietnam's fresh and crunchy specialties is **gỏi cuốn** ❷ — a spring roll made of rice paper filled with young vegetables, herbs, tofu, shrimp or meat.

TƯƠNG XÀO
Dipping sauce made of soy paste with garlic and chilli

TƯƠNG ĐẬU PHỘNG
Peanut dipping sauce

NƯỚC MẮM PHA
Fish-based dipping sauce

THE NGÃ BẢY FLOATING
MARKET ON THE MEKONG RIVER DELTA

SUPERGREENS

▶ In Vietnamese cuisine, fresh **herbs** ❿ are essential. These vibrant greens help bring out the flavours in a dish and add a fresh aroma. Meals are often accompanied by lots of fragrant leaves.

These can be eaten on their own or used as wraps for meat skewers ❾.

PERILLA — The underside of the Vietnamese variety of this herb is purple.

THAI BASIL — This common herb is the most popular topping for phở soup.

PEPPER LEAF

BÁNH CHUỐI NƯỚNG

Banana cake
Baking time: ⏱ 1 hour
Preparation: ⏱ 20 minutes. 6× ▦

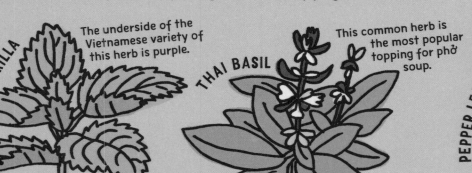

2 tbsp butter (30 g)

4 bananas

2 tbsp sugar

salt

2 tsp vanilla extract

1 can coconut milk (400 g)

2 tbsp sweet condensed milk

6 slices white bread

A rare Vietnamese variety of short, plump bananas are used to make bánh chuối nướng; they turn a reddish colour when cooked! Regular bananas work just as well in this recipe, but make sure they are very ripe.

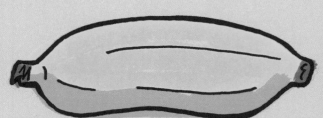

1 Melt 2 tablespoons of butter in a small pot. Peel the bananas and slice into pieces ½ cm thick. Put these slices in a bowl, along with 2 tablespoons of sugar, a pinch of salt and the vanilla extract. Gently mix the ingredients together.

2 Take a second bowl and whip the coconut milk together with the condensed milk. Cut the crusts off the slices of bread and add them to the milky mixture. Set aside for 15 minutes. Heat your oven to 170°C.

FRUITY ARRAY

▶ Along with fresh vegetables, fruits are an important part of both sweet and savoury dishes. For a visitor, the sheer variety of fruit in Vietnam can be mind-boggling. Eaten in season, even plucked straight from the tree or bush, these fruits are bursting with flavour.

BREADFRUIT ⑱ — Native to India, the breadfruit is the largest fruit borne by a tree. Just one breadfruit can be up to 1 metre long and weigh up to 35 kilograms.

DRAGON FRUIT ⑬ — Originating in South America and also known as a 'pitaya', this fruit comes from the cactus family.

LONGAN ⑫ — Native to Southeast Asia, longan is Mandarin for 'dragon's eye'.

COCONUT ⑭ — Most likely originating in India and Melanesia, the coconut is known for its delicate white flesh hidden beneath a hard shell. The inside is also filled with refreshing coconut water.

MEXICAN CORIANDER Also known as cilantro, this herb is a popular garnish in Vietnamese dishes and often used to treat digestive issues.

VIETNAMESE MINT This is a popular addition to many local dishes.

An ideal ingredient in Vietnamese salads and gỏi cuốn.

RICE PADDY HERB (NGO OM)

VIETNAMESE CORIANDER This goes wonderfully in salads.

3 Use part of the melted butter to grease a cake pan (approx. 20 x 20 cm). Set a few banana slices aside and add the rest to the milky-bread mixture, stirring gently.

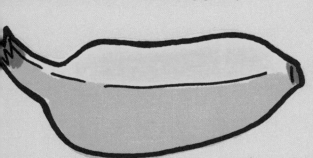

4 Pour the mixture into the cake pan and use the bananas you set aside to decorate the top. Bake for 15 minutes. Pour the rest of the melted butter on top and bake for another 45 minutes.

5 When the cake is just about done, set the oven to 'grilling' mode to toast the bananas on top. Remove the cake and allow to cool.

Uyen makes bánh chuối nướng for her grandchildren every time they visit.

MANGOSTEEN Native to Malaysia, this fruit is considered among the tastiest in the world.

RAMBUTAN The name of this fruit in Vietnamese is *chôm chôm*, which means 'raggedy hair'. This furry fruit is native to Southeast Asia.

BANANA Domesticated in Papua New Guinea thousands of years ago, today there are numerous varieties of this staple fruit that differ in size, colour, taste and the ways they can be eaten.

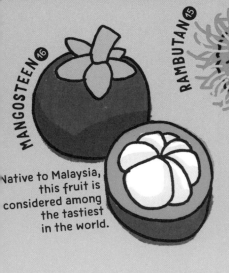

MANGO Mangoes come from South Asia, and are one of the most popular tropical fruits.

DURIAN Native to Malaysia, this prickly item is famous for its appalling smell. Some hate this rotten-smelling fruit, but some love it.

INDONESIA
SWEET, SOUR, FIERY, SAVOURY AND BITTER

- Indonesia is an archipelago made up of 17,508 islands. Situated between two oceans, three tectonic plates push against each other in this region, causing hundreds of earthquakes and volcanoes ❸. At least 100 of the latter are ready to blow at any moment.
- Indonesia's history is a turbulent one. Each wave of occupiers brought along new customs and religions. Trade relations with China, India, Europe and the Arab world brought rice, peanuts, chilli peppers and fermented soy, all now staples of Indonesian cuisine.

- The nation's fraught history and complex geography has resulted in great diversity. There are as many as 300 different ethnic groups living in Indonesia, and over 700 languages and dialects are spoken. This diverse group also observe many different religious practices. It is no wonder then that the country's customs and culinary traditions are wide-ranging.
- The different kinds of Indonesian cuisine are linked through their common approach to cooking: sweetness often comes with a sour kick, along with a dash of heat and bitterness.

SOYBEANS AND SPORES
- People have been making **tempeh** ⑫ for hundreds of years, and yet for some, the recipe might sound like something straight out of a science fiction novel.

Rinse the soybeans.

Boil them in water.

OPOR AYAM
Chicken in coconut sauce
Preparation and cooking time: 🕐🕐 2 hours,
5 × 🍲

3 tbsp vegetable oil

2 stalks lemongrass

2 kaffir lime leaves

3 laurel leaves

1 tbsp tamarind paste

1 tsp brown sugar

1–1½ kg chicken

3 cups coconut milk (750 ml)

salt

Marinade

⅓ cup peanuts (50 g)

1 tsp coriander seed

½ tsp cumin seed

¾ tsp turmeric powder

½ tsp chilli powder

5 cloves of garlic

7 small shallots

4 cm galang stem

5 tbsp water

salt

The traditional version of this recipe calls for candlenuts, but as they are not as widely available in the rest of the world, peanuts can be used instead.

1 Toast the nuts in a dry pan and set aside. Then toast the coriander and cumin seeds. In a blender, whizz all three together alongside the remaining marinade ingredients.

2 In a large pot, heat the vegetable oil. Add the marinade and allow it to cook for 2 minutes.

UNIQUE FILLINGS
- Rice ⑩ is the most common accompaniment to most Indonesian meals, however not every island has the resources to cultivate enough of it. So, many people turn to sago and taro. Much like other starches*, they don't have a particularly interesting flavour on their own, but they fill an empty belly quickly.

* See more about starches on page 102.

SAGO ⑥
This is a thick, relatively tasteless paste made from sago palm stems. It can also be made from other palms, including date palms.

TARO ⑪
Also known as eddo or dasheen, taro is easy to cultivate and has been around for thousands of years. To eat taro, the bulbs must be peeled and cooked, although certain recipes do call for taro leaves and the softer parts of the stem.

▸ Tempeh is a protein-filled block of goodness. It is easy to make at home and simple to store. It can be cut up and fried, added to a stew, or eaten raw.

▸ As is the case with other soy products*, tempeh must go through a fermentation process, which breaks down the protein contained in the soy and makes it digestible for our gut. A special type of mould is used in the process, which keeps the block of tempeh firm and provides the characteristic flavour and texture.

* More on page 16.

3 Peel the shells.

4 Mix in the mould spores to start the fermentation process.

5 Form the mixture into bars and pack into bags.

6 After fermenting for 24–36 hours, your tempeh is ready!

3 Split each lemongrass stalk and add to the pot, along with the lime, laurel leaves, tamarind paste, sugar and salt. Cook for a few more minutes.

4 Add the chicken and continue cooking for several more minutes. Add the coconut milk.

5 Cover the mixture and cook for 1–2 hours, until the chicken is tender.

6 Add sugar and salt to taste. Serve over rice.

Agus often prepares opor ayam for his friends.

FOWL ABUNDANCE

▸ Apart from pork and fish, **poultry** ⑧ is among the most popular meat consumed by human beings worldwide. Every year, 20 billion chickens end up on our plates.

▸ The average person eats about 150 eggs a year. The record-holders in this category are the Chinese, who eat at least one egg per day, which adds up to a minimum of 1.5 billion eggs a day, in China alone.

▸ Chickens are an especially important part of the Indonesian diet, particularly in summer, when the strong winds and rains make fishing very difficult.

The first chickens were domesticated about 8,000 years ago. Based on genetic research, we know that their primitive ancestor is the red junglefowl, which originated in Southeast Asia.

Red junglefowl (male)

(female)

SOUR

▶ There are two plants in particular that bring out the characteristic sour flavour of Indonesian dishes: **tamarind** ⑨, which originated in Africa, and **lemongrass** ②, a fibrous stalk that is native to Southeast Asia.

▶ The tamarind tree is a tall evergreen tree that bears long pods full of tough seeds. The seeds are surrounded by a soft brown pulp that is used to add a tangy note to certain foods or sweet drinks.

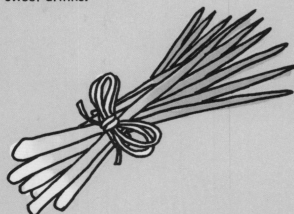

▶ Lemongrass lends a citrusy aroma to various sauces and roasted fish and poultry dishes. Typically, only the green part of the stem is used. Its popularity is due to its versatility — it can even be enjoyed as a steaming cup of herbal tea.

SWEET

▶ **Palm sugar** proves the perfect dose of sweetness for all types of dishes and desserts, while the **coconut** provides a gentle sweetness to Indonesian cooking.

▶ Sugar is produced from the juice ⑤ squeezed from the flowers and stalks of different varieties of palm plants. It is boiled until most of the liquid has evaporated, leaving behind a thick paste.

▶ Coconut milk is pressed directly from the sweet white pulp inside the tough shell of this fruit ④*.

* Find out more about coconuts on page 30.

SPICY

▶ **Galangal** ① offers a spicy, peppery note, while **sambal** delivers a truly fiery kick ⑦ ⑯.

▶ Galangal is a root. Otherwise known by its botanical name *Alpinia galgant*, it is related to the ginger family. It is typically used in thick soups, stews and sauces. The most popular variety used in Indonesian cooking is called 'laos'.

▶ Sambal is a name that not only stands for a spicy chilli-based condiment, but also a number of Indonesian dishes that combine spicy, salty and citrusy flavours in one.

SAVOURY

▶ The dark sauce known as **kecap manis**⑭ (and the thick paste widely known as **terasi**⑮) both add an essential dash of savoury flavour to any dish.

▶ Kecap manis is the Indonesian twist on soy sauce and, much like its Chinese cousin*, it is made of soy, but the difference lies in its sweetness. Thanks to the addition of palm sugar and a shorter fermentation time, a sweeter and stickier sauce is produced.

* More about soy sauce on page 23.

▶ Terasi is a thick dry paste made of fermented shrimp. Unlike other condiments, it is not to be eaten raw — instead it is added during the cooking process.

GADO GADO

Salad with peanut sauce dressing
⏱ 45 minutes, 4×🍲

Feel free to add your own favourite vegetables to the mix.

 4 potatoes

 4 eggs

 200 g tempeh (or tofu)

 2 pak choi cabbages

 2 handfuls of fresh spinach

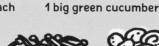 1 big green cucumber

 2 handfuls of cooked green beans

 2 handfuls of raw bean sprouts

prawn crackers

·········· Bumbu kacang peanut dressing ··········

 1 cup peanut butter (280 g)

 2 garlic cloves

 2 cm galang root

 ½ chilli

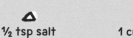 2 tsp brown sugar

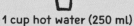 3 tbsp lime juice

½ tsp salt

1 cup hot water (250 mL)

1 Boil the potatoes with their skins, then peel them. When cool, cut into slices.

2 Hard boil the eggs and cut into fourths. Cut the tempeh or tofu into slices and fry until golden.

3 Scald the pak choi and cut into thick chunks. Cut the cucumber into slices and arrange on a plate with the remaining vegetables.

4 Use a blender to mix all the ingredients for the dressing together.

Siti always serves up a yummy gado gado.

BITTER

▶ A dash of bitter is often provided by the aptly named fruit known as **bitter melon** ⑬, a cousin of the pumpkin. Its fruit is harvested before it is fully ripe and used in cooking.

UNITED STATES OF AMERICA
AS YOU LIKE IT

- The United States is a vast country with a diverse climate. When we think of American cuisine, we often think of hamburgers, but American cuisine reflects the great diversity of its people, its rich landscape and its tumultuous history.
- The European colonisation of North America began 400 years ago. Settlers brought over grains, plants and livestock from their lands, as well as lots of recipes.
- The settlers were keen to use the natural resources that they had at their disposal, including corn❹, beans, pumpkin❿, the (tough to domesticate) turkey❼, shellfish❽⓱, and even tropical fruits (towards the southern coast)⓬.
- This smorgasbord of ingredients gave way to a number of unique dishes that have become a signature of great American cooking. For instance, the type of soup known as chowder, and crab cakes, have their roots in England. Louisiana-style cooking took its early cues from French cuisine, while the Italians delivered their famous pizza⓭ and pasta. The Dutch added a sweet touch with their waffles and an early version of the classic donut⓫. Jewish people from Poland brought bagels⓰, while Germans prepared their own pretzels⓮ and sausages — precursors of the famous New York hot dog⓯.
- Over the centuries, each new wave of immigration to the United States brought in new customs and recipes. Certain dishes retained their original guise, while others have evolved dramatically in their taste, their presentation, or both!

CHILLI CON CARNE
A bowl of beef, tomatoes and beans with a spicy kick.

NACHOS
Crunchy tortilla* triangles that are either baked or fried, served with toppings such as cheese, salsa and jalapeño peppers.

* More on page 42.

TEX-MEX❸
- The state of Texas is known as the cowboy capital of the U.S. and is a rancher's dream. A third of the residents of this state have connections to Mexico and other Spanish-speaking nations. So, it's no wonder that **Tex-Mex** cuisine has flourished here with its winning combination of Mexican classics (like the tortilla) and American obsessions (like oozing, melted cheese).

BARBECUE❺
A tender hunk of meat glazed in a special sauce and smoked on low heat for hours is an American tradition.

Americans have outdoor barbecues to celebrate most special occasions and national holidays, especially the 4th of July.

POPCORN❷
These puffed-up* kernels of corn have been eaten by the native inhabitants of North and South America for over 5,000 years.

The first popcorn machine was installed at a movie theatre in 1938. From this moment on, popcorn (best topped with melted butter) has become a cinematic staple and a symbol of pop culture.

* When popcorn kernels are heated, the water inside them turns into steam and the pressure causes the shell to explode. Their tasty insides pop out, giving us popcorn.

HAMBURGER ⏱ 30 minutes, 4 × 🍔
Minced beef patty

1 tomato	1 small red onion	2 pickles	iceberg lettuce	600 g minced beef (not fully lean)
4 tbsp oil	salt and pepper	4 hamburger buns	2 tbsp butter (30 g)	mustard, ketchup, mayonnaise

1 Slice the tomato, onion and pickle. Tear or cut the lettuce into big pieces.

2 Shape the minced beef into 4 flat patties. Take care not to squeeze them too much.

3 Pour the oil into a frying pan. When it is hot enough, add the patties (they should sizzle right away). Sprinkle them with salt and pepper and then fry for 4–5 minutes on each side until they are fully browned.

4 Cut the buns in half and spread butter inside. Warm up a dry pan and set the buns down on the buttered side. Heat until they are golden and crispy.

5 On the golden side of the bun, arrange the lettuce, then the beef patty, a few slices of onion, a slice of tomato and pickle. Add mustard, ketchup and mayonnaise and set the other half of the bun on top.

Makayla presses a small dimple into the middle of the patty.

This prevents the burger shrinking whilst frying.

FAST AND CHEAP
► White Castle was the first fast-food franchise in the U.S. About a century has passed since the fast-food revolution began.
► **Drive-in** restaurants also became popular, where meals were delivered right to the customer's car. Soon enough, servers were equipped with roller skates to speed up delivery known as 'carhops'. Then came the advent of the **drive-thru ❶** where motorists could order a meal through a microphone and speaker, and drive up to another window to pick it up.
► Today's **fast-food** chains mostly produce cheap meals of relatively low nutritional value, though healthier choices are becoming more popular. Sadly though, not many places use carhops anymore!

CHOP SUEY
杂碎

Legend has it that chop suey was first invented as a dish over 150 years ago by a Chinese chef living in the U.S. He had run out of most of his provisions so made a meal out of whatever ingredients were still available. He named the dish, **'tsap seui'**, which in Chinese means 'various leftovers'.

Urban legends aside, chop suey is the American version of a Chinese dish that originated in Guangzhou.

The U.S. version consists of finely sliced meat and vegetables fried in a wok.

SWIFT ADAPTATION
► The first Chinese immigrants came to the U.S. nearly two centuries ago. Chinese chefs began to adapt their recipes to local tastes,

FORTUNE COOKIES
These crispy crescent-shaped treats have a surprise inside — a tiny slip of paper with a fortune written on it.

These cookies have been popular since the early 20th century. They are thought to have originated in Kyoto, Japan — it was the Japanese who brought them over to the U.S.

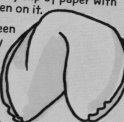

However, during the Second World War, when Japan was considered an enemy of the state, many people of Japanese descent were taken to internment camps, and Japanese restaurants and bakeries were closed. Meanwhile, the production of fortune cookies was taken over by people of Chinese descent and soon became a staple in many Chinese restaurants.

In the 1990s, there was an attempt to market fortune cookies to Chinese consumers, but they were considered 'too American'.

but the new twists on tradition were still sold to Americans as classic Chinese cuisine.

AMERICAN ALL-STARS

STUFFED TURKEY / PUMPKIN PIE

These are two of the most popular dishes enjoyed by Americans on the national holiday of **Thanksgiving 9**. Turkeys and pumpkins are both native to North America and were first eaten by the native people of the continent and then later adopted as autumn and winter staples by settlers from Europe.

CHOWDER

This thick and hearty soup is chock-full of seafood and cream, with a handful of crackers to thicken it even more. It was brought to America over 250 years ago with the first **English settlers**.

BAGELS 16

These doughy rolls with a characteristic hole in the middle were invented by Polish Jews more than 400 years ago.

They arrived in the U.S. much later as part of the wave of Jewish immigration. Fragrantly yeasty, plain or sprinkled with salt, poppyseed or sesame, bagels were a quick hit, especially as a tasty base for sandwiches.

DONUTS 11

This round pastry, which often comes with a hole in the middle, can come with a range of toppings of all kinds and sweet fillings.

The original donut was based on the **Dutch** olykoeks* — in other words, a ball of dough deep-fried in oil.

* In Dutch, the word means 'oily cakes'.

HOT DOG 15

Tucked into a long toasted bun and smeared in ketchup, mustard, sauerkraut or pickles, **frankfurters*** are an easy meal on the go.

These thin smoked sausages filled with a tender minced filling were introduced to the U.S. by **German** immigrants. A century ago, people were already eating frankfurters in the form of hot dogs across big U.S. cities, but it wasn't until businessman **Nathan Handwerker's** efforts that they became famous.

In 1916, Nathan opened up his first hot dog stall on Coney Island in New York. His hot dogs were so popular that Nathan's soon expanded into a chain known across all 50 states and even across the world.

* More on page 62.

CRAWFISH BISQUE

Another hearty soup typically served with rice, bisque originates from French cooking. It's full of herbs, crabmeat (or other seafood) and thickened with bread.

Crawfish 8 are a widely popular ingredient in **Cajun cooking**, which originates in Louisiana, where seafood is plentiful. Every year, the city of Breaux Bridge hosts a festival dedicated entirely to these scrumptious crustaceans.

GUMBO 6

Gumbo is also from Louisiana. It is a thick stew made of crabs, oysters, chicken or sausage, though vegetarian options are also popular. 'Roux' is flour slow-cooked in oil, and is key to any gumbo recipe. It is added alongside filé powder*, or **okra**, to ensure the sauce is rich and thick.

Gumbo is an ideal example of America's distinctive cultural mix. It reflects the influence drawn from the customs of the native **Choctaw** tribe, **Cajuns** (the descendants of French settlers in the region), **Germans** and **Creoles** (whose own traditions blend elements of French, Spanish, African and Caribbean cultures).

* Filé powder is a seasoning made of dried sassafras leaves.

okra slice

PEANUT BUTTER PIE
A creamy peanut dessert

Baking: 🕐 30 minutes
Preparation: 🕐 60 minutes, 8×🍰

··········· Pastry crust ···········

| 1½ cups flour (250 g) | 1 tsp sugar | big pinch of salt | 80 g chilled butter | 60 g chilled margarine | 7-8 tbsp ice-cold water |

··········· Filling ···········

| 300 g cream cheese | 1 cup peanut butter (280 g) | ¾ cup powdered sugar (90 g) | 50 g melted butter | 1 tsp vanilla extract (optional) | 1½ cups 36% heavy cream (375 ml) | 2 tbsp powdered sugar |

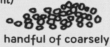
handful of coarsely chopped nuts

1 In a large bowl, combine the flour, sugar and salt. Cut the chilled butter and margarine into cubes and shake the bowl to mix them with the flour, then gently use your fingers to create breadcrumbs. Slowly add cold water until the dough is firm enough to roll into a ball. Flatten it out a bit and cover in foil. Put in the fridge for 30 minutes to chill.

2 Heat the oven to 200°C. Roll out the dough and set it into a pie dish about 25 cm in diameter. Bake for 20-30 minutes, until the bottom is golden. Set aside to cool.

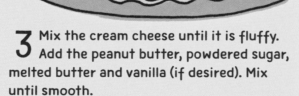

3 Mix the cream cheese until it is fluffy. Add the peanut butter, powdered sugar, melted butter and vanilla (if desired). Mix until smooth.

4 Whip the cream, adding the remaining 2 tbsp powdered sugar.

5 Take half the whipped cream and mix gently into the peanut butter-cream cheese mixture. Spoon into the cooled pie crust.

6 Top the the pie with the remaining whipped cream and decorate with the nuts. Serve straightaway, or, for the very best taste, chill it overnight.

Michael loves a big helping of peanut butter pie.

THE NUTTY INVENTOR

▶ The indigenous people of South America started cultivating **peanuts** around 4,000 years ago, but peanuts didn't make it over to Europe until the Spanish colonisers brought them back home. Later, the Portuguese brought them over to Africa. Many decades later, peanuts were brought back across the Atlantic on slave ships — this time to North America.

▶ At first, peanuts were mainly used for animal feed. And even though the Aztecs* had already discovered the allure of peanut butter so many millennia before, the American colonisers were not so easily convinced.

▶ It wasn't until **George Washington Carver** that peanuts regained their rightful glory. Carver was a widely recognised botanist and inventor of the early 20th century. He urged farmers to alternate their cotton crops with sweet potatoes and peanuts to maintain the soil and ensure bountiful harvests.

▶ Carver also came up with a book of 105 tasty peanut-based recipes.

* Find out more about the Aztecs on page 40.

George Washington Carver

MEXICO
CORN, CHILLI AND PAINTED SKULLS

Pyramid of Calakmul

MAYAN CIVILISATION

Pyramid of Kukulcan

FIRST TRIBES

- Around 9,000 years ago, the inhabitants of modern-day Mexico ① mostly ate the plants that grew around them: corn ④, beans, pumpkins, tomatoes, cassava ⑥, chilli peppers ② and avocado ③. They also hunted mammals, fish and turtles and ate some kinds of insects.
- About 4,000 years ago, the Mayans ⑤ founded a great civilisation, now famous for its architecture, writing system and calendar. The Mayans also developed agriculture and livestock breeding.
- About 1,000 years later, the Aztec Empire began ⑭. Their capital was Tenochtitlán ⑮, situated on an island on Lake Texcoco (Mexico City is built on its ruins).
- In 1521, the Spanish conquistador Hernán Cortés overthrew the Aztec Empire. His invasion brought catastrophe, death and a lethal strain of smallpox to the region, and also the introduction of European goods.
- Mexican culture and cuisine evolved from influences by both the local people and colonisers. Wheat, rice, cattle and pigs ⑯ were introduced to the local diet alongside corn, beans and chilli.

CLEANING CORN

- The Mayans introduced **nixtamalization** ⑪, to agriculture — a way of processing corn to remove toxins. This also makes it easier to mill the corn into flour and make tortillas and other corn-based products.

1 Separate the kernels.

2 Soak and boil the corn. → alkaline solution

3 Grind into flour.

Ancient corn had a cob that was only 25 millimetres long ④.

By selectively cultivating the grains from the longest cobs, the Mayans created varieties that were longer — and had more kernels per cob! ④

Today, about a billion tonnes of corn are produced each year. Only a small proportion is grown for human consumption. Other types of corn are grown for oil or syrup, or added to pet food or other products.

TACOS

Folded, stuffed tortillas
🕐 45 minutes, 8× 🌮

Señora Alejandra has a secret recipe.

 500 g beef   1 small onion   juice of ½ lime   4 tbsp olive oil   7–8 tortillas *See recipe on next page.*   salt

········· Toppings ·········

See recipes over the next few pages.

lettuce leaves   1 onion   2–3 bunches coriander, chopped   2 limes   tomato salsa   guacamole

1 Chop the meat into slices, add the chopped onion and lime juice. Mix together, then marinate for 20 minutes in the fridge.

2 Wash the lettuce and cut into strips. Dice the other onion. Cut the limes into quarters.

3 Heat the oil in a frying pan. Salt the meat and cook on a medium heat for 10 minutes or until the liquid has evaporated.

AZTEC EMPIRE

Tenochtitlán, ancient capital of the Aztec Empire

Montezuma II

Hernán Cortés

THE SPANISH CONQUEST

SWALLOWING FIRE

▶ There are countless varieties of hot peppers ❷, around the world. They all get their fiery kick from **capsaicin**, a chemical compound that causes a burning sensation in our mouths when we eat chillies.

▶ When we've had an especially fiery chilli pepper, it doesn't really help to drink water as the capsaicin cannot be dissolved. It's better to have a glass or milk or some ice cream.

Because birds have fewer taste buds, they can consume lots of chilli peppers. This helps to spread their seeds.

Elephants can't stand hot peppers, but they enjoy eating other vegetables. Farmers in Asia and Africa line their fields with chilli pepper plants to repel the gentle giants and keep them from trampling crops.

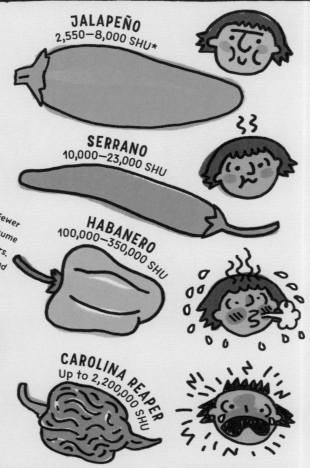

JALAPEÑO
2,550–8,000 SHU*

SERRANO
10,000–23,000 SHU

HABANERO
100,000–350,000 SHU

CAROLINA REAPER
Up to 2,200,000 SHU

* The Scoville Scale is a way of measuring the spiciness of chilli peppers. Measured in Scoville Heat Units (SHUs), the scale is named for its inventor, Wilbur Scoville. The higher the SHU, the hotter the pepper.

THE WHOLE PACKAGE

▶ A perfectly ripe **avocado** ❸ is a real delicacy. This doesn't mean that tougher ones should go straight in the bin though!

▶ Each and every fruit on Earth releases a chemical known as ethylene*, which speeds up the ripening process. An avocado picked before it is ripe might therefore still soften within the next few days.

▶ When we don't feel like waiting so long, one shortcut is to place the unripe avocado in a paper bag with a fully ripe apple or banana.

The hass is the most popular variety of avocado.

* Certain fruits (such as strawberries) stop releasing ethylene as soon as they are picked.

---

4 Fill your tortilla with meat and toppings. Add the salsa and guacamole. Drizzle with lime juice and fold in half to serve.

TOMATO SALSA

A spicy, tangy dip. ⏱ 10 minutes. 1×🥣

2 small tomatoes

½ red onion

big handful of chopped coriander (also known as cilantro)

½ chopped chilli pepper

¼ tsp oregano

2 pinches of ground cumin

salt

juice from ½ lime

1 Dice the tomatoes and onion and add to a bowl.

2 Add the coriander, chilli pepper, oregano, cumin and salt. Drizzle over the lime juice and mix all the ingredients together.

Find out how to make guacamole on the next page.

DARK TREASURE

▸ The Mayans valued cocoa⑩ highly. The Aztec leader Montezuma apparently drank a cup of bitter cocoa spiced with chilli and vanilla⑨ every day. The dried cocoa beans⑫ were brought in from far away and were so valuable they were used as a form of currency.

▸ This diagram shows how many cocoa beans each item is worth:

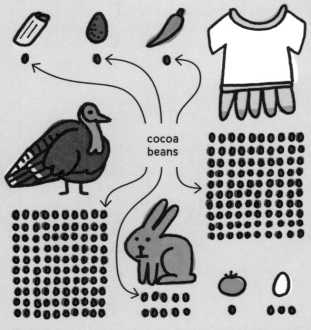

cocoa beans

CHOCOLATE DREAM

▸ The first bar of chocolate was manufactured about 150 years ago when a machine was developed to separate the fat solids from the cocoa.

▸ This invention reduced the cost of chocolate production and soon the whole world had access to the delicious sweet treat.

1 Harvest the cocoa pods.

2 Scoop the pulp and beans out.

3 Ferment the beans alongside the pulp.

4 Dry the beans.

5 Roast the beans.

6 Crush the roasted beans.

7 Separate the shells. The wind blows the shells away.

8 Grind the beans.

9 Press the cocoa solids.

cocoa mass

cocoa butter

The pressed cocoa solids are then milled into a powder.

cocoa solids + cocoa powder + sugar → dark chocolate

cocoa solids + sugar + milk → milk chocolate

cocoa butter + milk + sugar → white chocolate

GUACAMOLE

Avocado dip ⏱ 10 minutes, 1×🥣

3 ripe avocados

juice of ½ lime (optional)

½ small onion

½ chopped chilli (optional)

2 tbsp chopped coriander leaves

3 tbsp olive oil

salt and pepper

1 Cut the avocado in half, remove the stone and peel. Mash with a fork and add the lime juice.

2 Dice the onion and add to the mashed avocado, along with the chilli (if using), coriander, olive oil and season with salt and pepper. Combine the ingredients and serve right away.

🫙 To stop the guacamole turning brown, put it in a container, drizzle with lime juice, cover with plastic wrap and store in the fridge.

TORTILLA | CORN OR WHEAT

Round flatbread
⏱ 45 minutes, 8×🫓

🌽 To make corn tortillas, you need a type of corn flour called masa harina which has undergone nixtamalization⑪. Tortillas made from regular corn flour will simply fall apart.

🌾 You can also make tortillas out of wheat flour. Wheat was introduced to Mexico by Spanish colonisers.

OCTOBER 31,
NOVEMBER 1 AND 2

LUNCH ON THE GO

▶ **Street food** is a big part of Mexican culture. Everywhere, carts, stands and trucks offer their own spin on Mexican specialities.

ENCHILADA 22

A filled tortilla, rolled up and covered in sauce.

TORTA 23

A bun filled with grilled meat, avocado, chillies and tomatoes.

TACO 21

See the recipe on page 40.

A tortilla folded in half and filled with meat and toppings.

ATOLE 19

A hot drink made of corn flour 8 20, water and sugar.

TAMALE 17

The banana leaf is not edible.

Cornmeal dough stuffed with a meat mixture, then wrapped in a corn husk or banana leaf and steamed.

Tamales 17 were eaten by the Mayans and Aztecs 13 and are still popular today.

QUESADILLA 18

A toasted tortilla filled with melted cheese and other toppings.

HAPPY SKULLS

▶ **Día de los Muertos**, or 'Day of the Dead' is a three-day celebration of loved ones who have passed.

▶ People visit a cemetery 24 or gather at home around an **ofrenda** 27 — an altar filled with pictures and belongings of their loved ones, and foods, such as atole, tamales and sweetbread 25. Decorations in the shape of skulls 26, wreaths of marigolds 28, candles and merry skeleton figures are used. Other traditions include face painting or putting on costumes and masks 29 (similarly to Halloween!).

▶ The purpose of the festival is to let those on the other side know that the living remember them.

Some people believe that the spirits of the dead draw all the energy out of the food on the altar so that the living don't have to worry about gaining weight.

For the corn version:

2¼ cups nixtamalized corn flour (250 g)

1½ tsp salt

1⅓ cups water (330 ml)

For the wheat version:

2 cups wheat flour (280 g)

½ tsp baking powder

½ tsp salt

65 g margarine

½ cup warm water (125 ml)

1 Place the flour and salt in a large bowl. For wheat tortillas, add the baking powder. Mix.

2 For wheat tortillas, add the margarine (chopped into cubes). Mash it into the flour so that the mixture forms clumps.

3 Gradually add water, using a fork to mix. Use your hands to form the dough.

4 Divide the dough into 8 parts. Roll them out between sheets of plastic wrap

(or you can use a plastic bag). Make discs around 20 cm in diameter and 2 mm thick.

5 Heat the pan until it is very hot and dry fry the tortillas on a medium heat for 3–4 minutes on each side.

PERU
FAKE GRAINS AND RIGHTEOUS ROOTS

MACHU PICCHU

▶ Humans appeared in what is now Peru around 14,000 years ago. The valleys of the Andes and the Pacific coast were home to the Norte Chico people and also the Nazca people. Now known as the Nazca lines, the Nazcas are famous for the enormous artworks they created in the desert sands.

▶ 800 years ago, the Inca Empire ❷ was founded in Peru — one of the greatest civilisations in history. This empire was another victim of the Spanish invaders ⓫ who arrived in South America 300 years later. The Europeans not only had more powerful weapons, but they also brought lethal diseases with them. The colonisers destroyed the Inca culture and architecture ❹, and few traces of their empire remain.

▶ Peruvian cuisine today unites age-old local traditions with Spanish, African and Asian influences. There are also regional differences based on the diversity in climate between the hot valleys, cool mountain tops and tropical rainforests of the country.

PAPAS RELLENAS
Potato croquettes
⏱ 1 hour, 14×◯

1½ kg potatoes	1 tbsp raisins	1 small onion	2 garlic cloves	2 eggs · oil
1 tsp tomato purée	½ tsp sweet chilli pepper	¼ tsp ground cumin	¼ tsp chilli powder	
150 g ground beef	a handful of black olives	salt and pepper	wheat flour	

1 Peel the potatoes, cut into chunks and boil in salted water until soft. Drain, mash and set aside to cool.

2 Scald the raisins and set aside for 10 minutes, then drain. Dice the onion and garlic. Hard boil an egg.

3 Cook the onion until soft. Add the garlic and cook for another minute. Add the tomato purée, raisins and spices. Fry for 3 minutes.

Llamas are strong and plucky. If threatened, their powerful kicks can kill coyotes and foxes.

Long ears rounded at the tip

LLAMA

GUINEA PIG (cavia)

Short, pointy ears

Alpacas are curious and more gentle-natured.

Weighs up to 250 kg

Weighs up to 85 kg

ALPACA

FURRY FRIENDS

▶ The inhabitants of Peru had been raising llamas ❸, alpacas ❺ and guinea pigs ❻ for thousands of years before the European colonisation of South America. Llamas and alpacas were used to carry heavy loads and for their warm wool, while guinea pigs were tasty snacks! Even in the Andes today, open-air markets sell skewers of grilled rodents ⓱ and llama meat as well as cosy alpaca wool sweaters.

Rénan is a big fan of pappas rellenas!

4 Add the meat and cook for 10 more minutes, stirring from time to time. Take the pan off the heat and set aside.

5 Coarsely chop the olives and the boiled eggs and add to the meat. Season and leave to cool.

6 Scoop up a handful of potato and flatten it against your palm. Add a teaspoon of filling then cover with another layer of potato. Form into an oblong oval shape, dip it into the whisked egg yolk and then coat with flour.

7 Heat some oil in a pan and when hot, fry the croquettes until they are golden on both sides. Drain on a plate covered with paper towels.

8 Enjoy hot or cold, with a garnish of salsa criolla (see below for recipe).

SALSA CRIOLLA
Onion garnish, ⏱ 15 minutes, 6×🍲

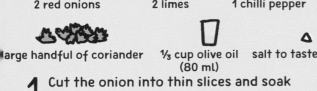

2 red onions   2 limes   1 chilli pepper

large handful of coriander   ⅓ cup olive oil (80 ml)   salt to taste

1 Cut the onion into thin slices and soak in cold water for 15 minutes.

2 Squeeze the limes. Finely dice the chilli and coriander. Mix all the ingredients together and serve.

LUSCIOUS AND PLENTIFUL
▸ Peru is a fruitarian's* paradise! There are so many different types of juicy fruits available that it's impossible to get bored.

*Fruitarians eat only raw fruit, seeds and nuts.

CAMU CAMU 20
An acidic fruit packed with vitamin C.

PACAY 22
The pod is not edible.

The edible part is the soft, slightly vanilla-flavoured pulp surrounding the beans inside.

LUCUMA 24
The sweet flesh is similar to pumpkin.

PERUVIAN GROUNDCHERRY 19
The husk is discarded before eating.
An acidic fruit also known as the 'goldenberry'.

PRICKLY PEAR 23
A refreshing fruit from the cactus family.

CHERIMOYA 18
A sweet and creamy fruit, like a mix of banana, pear and pineapple.

PASSION FRUIT 21
The gooey pulp and seeds scooped from the middle give a surprising sweet-and-tangy taste.

FRESH FISH DISH
▸ **Ceviche** 12 is a method of marinating raw fish in lime or lemon juice with a dash of salt and onion. It's especially popular on the coast.
▸ It is typically served as a starter or as a bigger meal along with a helping of corn and sweet potatoes. There are many ways to serve ceviche and they're all delicious! Ceviche is the national dish of Peru.

The acidity of the citrus helps to break down the protein in the fish, the same way cooking does.

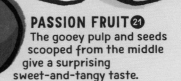
Fresh fish and citrus is the key to ceviche!

Francisco Pizarro

Atahualpa

ALFAJORES
Sandwiched cookies
Preparation: ⏱ 1 hour
Baking: ⏱ 15 minutes, 15×🍪

200 g softened butter

⅓ cup powdered sugar (50 g)

1 egg

1¾ cup flour (260 g)

▽ salt

¾ can dulce de leche (380 g)

Manjar blanco means 'white deliciousness' in Spanish and is a sweet creamy fudge, similar to dulce de leche*.

You can also make the sauce yourself. In a pan, heat 600 ml of 30% fat cream with 150 g of sugar. Stir occasionally over a low heat for around 2 hours, until the liquid thickens and turns a golden caramel colour.

1 Cut the butter into chunks and place in a bowl with the sugar. Blend for 3 minutes until fluffy.

* Dulce de leche means 'sweet (made) of milk' and is popular in other Spanish-speaking countries.

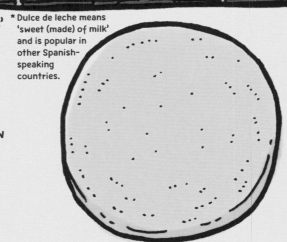

POTATO PARTY
▶ Potatoes are so plentiful in Peru that in the Andes alone there are 3,000 varieties.

In South America, potatoes have been a staple for over 7,000 years but they

only became popular in Europe about 250 years ago.

ROOTS RULE
▶ The potato may be the king of starchy vegetables, but there are plenty of others that can be dug out of the earth and enjoyed, too.

OCA 9 16

These tubers can be eaten raw, but after they are dried, they develop a pleasing sweetness. When boiled, their flavour and texture resemble that of a potato.

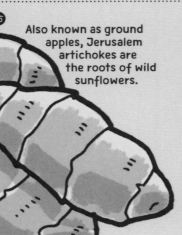
JERUSALEM ARTICHOKE 15

Also known as ground apples, Jerusalem artichokes are the roots of wild sunflowers.

ULLUCO 10 14

These small, colourful tubers can be cooked without peeling.

2 Add the egg, a pinch of salt and the flour. Combine the ingredients to form a firm ball. Cover with plastic foil and chill in the fridge for 30 minutes.

3 Heat the oven to 180°C. Roll out the chilled dough to about 4 mm in thickness. Use a glass to cut out discs about 6 cm in diameter.

4 Arrange the cookies on baking paper and gently spear them with a fork. Bake for 15 minutes, until golden.

5 Once cooled, spread the creamy fudge between two cookies and sprinkle with powdered sugar.

Rodrigo and Alessandra always bake alfajores for their mother's birthday.

FROZEN GOODS

▸ **Chuño** 13 is a type of processed potato. The ancient method of production involved exposing a certain type of frost-resistant potato to extreme cold at night and warm sunlight during the day. Sometimes, excess liquid is also squeezed out of the potatoes by stepping on them 1. Once processed, the potatoes can be stored for a long time.

▸ Chuños provided much-needed sustenance to Incan warriors as they were sweet, filling and could be taken on long journeys.

Chuño again?

Yes, yum!

GORGEOUS GRAINS

▸ Cereals are a type of grass whose seeds are quite rich in starch (a type of plant sugar). Other types of plants produce a similar type of grain and are known are **pseudocereals**. They have been a staple of the Peruvian diet for thousands of years.

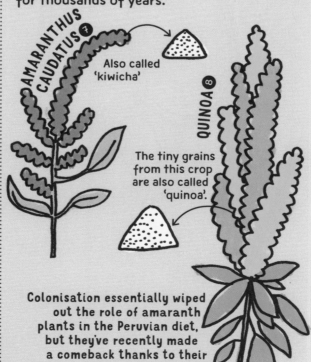

AMARANTHUS CAUDATUS 7

Also called 'kiwicha'

QUINOA 8

The tiny grains from this crop are also called 'quinoa'.

Colonisation essentially wiped out the role of amaranth plants in the Peruvian diet, but they've recently made a comeback thanks to their amazing nutritional content.

CORN

▸ The Incas, much like the Mayans and Aztecs* in Mexico, ate a lot of corn. They also made it into a popular drink known as **chicha morada**.

▸ You can still buy chicha morada in Peru or even make it yourself. You just need to get your hands on the unique Peruvian variety of **purple corn** then add pineapple, quince, sugar, cloves, cinnamon and lime.

* See more on page 40.

BRAZIL
WILD JUNGLES, FUNKY NUTS AND EYE-CATCHING BERRIES

BRASÍLIA IS THE CAPITAL CITY.

▸ Brazil was originally made up of lots of different tribes. They lived off the resources provided by the tropical rainforests —hunting, fishing and cultivating local varieties of beans ❺. The first European to arrive on this land was Pedro Álvares Cabral, who claimed this territory in the name of the Portuguese king.

▸ Cabral's arrival was the start of a brutal campaign of colonial exploitation which saw the enslavement of the native populations and enslaved Africans brought over to work the land. Ingredients from Europe and Africa such as rice, olive oil, garlic, palm oil*, coconuts, beef and and pork all shaped Brazilian cuisine.

▸ When Brazil gained its independence around 200 years ago, waves of immigrants added their own influences. Famous for its delicious coffee ❶, grilled churrasco meat dishes ❸ and splendid tropical fruits, Brazil also boasts a cuisine that includes foods from all four corners of the world.

* See more about palm oil on page 100.

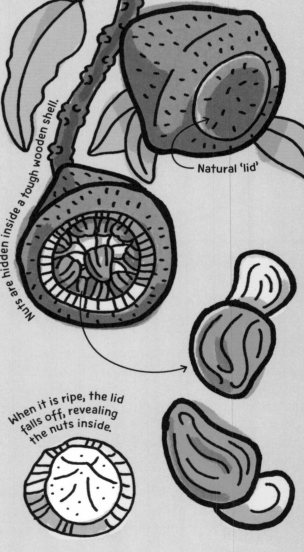

Nuts are hidden inside a tough wooden shell.

Natural 'lid'

When it is ripe, the lid falls off, revealing the nuts inside.

Cross-section of a cashew apple

Cashew nut

RED ALERT

▸ The **cashew** is native to Brazil. It makes a great roasted snack, and rich cashew butter is a fantastic base for vegan sauces, desserts and cheeses.

▸ A single cashew nut grows on the end of bitter cashew apples. These are the fruits of the *Anacardium occidentale* tree ❿.

▸ The shell of the cashew contains a substance that causes a skin reaction similar to that of poison ivy. Cashews are therefore always shelled before they are packed and sold.

TREASURE POTS

▸ **Paradise nuts** are the fruit of the tree known by the Latin name *Lecythis zabucajo* ⑮. They go bad almost immediately after being plucked from the tree so can only be enjoyed locally. They grow in tropical rainforests and are loved by humans and monkeys alike.

DANGEROUS DELIGHTS

▶ Another well-armoured nut is the **Brazil nut**. Brazil nut trees can grow up to 30 metres tall ⑪.

▶ When they are ripe, the hard and heavy brazil nut pods fall to the forest floor with incredible force, sometimes leaving a hole in the ground ⑬. Collecting Brazil nuts is therefore a game of roulette!

▶ Each pod holds between 10 and 25 Brazil nuts. These nuts can be stored and transported easily and are often found in packs of mixed nuts ⑭.

The entire nut and shell can weigh up to 2 kg.

The bitter coating

A peeled nut

The agouti is a type of nocturnal rodent. Aside from humans, it is the only animal able to crack a Brazil nut pod and get inside. They also bury the nuts, playing a vital role in the planting of new trees.

PÃO DE QUEIJO ②

Cheese bread
Preparation: ⏱ 20 minutes
Baking: ⏱ 40 minutes, 20–30 × ●

 ½ cup milk (125 ml)
 ½ cup water (125 ml)
 ¼ glass oil (62 ml)

 30 g butter
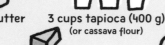 3 cups tapioca (400 g) (or cassava flour)
△ 2 tsp salt

70 g parmesan
◯ 1 egg

1 Add the milk, water and oil to a saucepan. Add the butter and bring to the boil. As soon as the butter has melted, remove from the heat.

2 In a large bowl, mix the tapioca and salt. Add the cheese and a beaten egg.

3 Add the tapioca mixture to the butter mixture. Blend together and knead into a dough. Heat the over to 200°C. Cover a tray with baking paper.

4 Shape the dough into small, walnut-sized balls. Arrange them on the baking sheet, taking care to leave enough space between them.

5 Bake for 40 minutes, until golden, and serve warm.

Maria often has pão de queijo for breakfast.

THE PERFECT BOUQUET

▶ Originally a delicacy enjoyed only in Central and South America, **pineapple** proved very popular with European colonisers and plantations were soon set up in other parts of the world. New ways of preserving the fruit were also found.

▶ For a long time, people outside of the Americas could only eat pineapple from a tin.

Today, the fruit can easily be transported. This does mean, however, that the fruit is often cut before it is ripe and doesn't taste as good as it should.

A single pineapple is actually made up of about 100 — sometimes even 200 — individual fruits that grow out of the same number of tiny flowers.

1 **2** **3** **4**

BRIGADEIRO
Chocolate truffles
Preparation: ⏱ 20 minutes
Chilling time: ⏲ 1 hour, 15–20×●

40 g butter

¾ can of dulce de leche (380 g)

4 tbsp cocoa powder

🍥 Brazilian **doce de leite** is a thick, caramel-like sauce that is made by cooking milk with sugar. You can prepare it yourself* or use ready-made dulce de leche from a tin.

*Find out how on page 46.

1 Melt the butter, then add the dulce de leche and mix. Add the cocoa gradually, whisking the entire time.

2 Cook on a low heat for 5–10 minutes, stirring until it begins to separate from the bottom of the pan.

3 Grease a plate with butter and pour the caramel mixture on top. Leave to cool in the fridge for an hour.

4 Cover your hands in butter and shape the chilled dulce de leche into walnut-sized balls. You could try covering them in cocoa or coconut shavings.

Antonio is helping himself to a handful of brigadeiros!

RISKY ROOTS

▸ **Cassava** (or manioc) is popular because it is so filling*. Resistant to drought, it grows quickly and doesn't have to be harvested right away. The root can even stay fresh in the ground for up to three years.

▸ The only problem is that cassava is also poisonous! Humans have therefore had to find ways to squeeze out the toxins.

▸ Cassava is typically made into a type of flour called tapioca. In Brazil, tapioca flour is used as a thickener and to make a local type of pancake ⑥. Tapioca pearls can also be used to make scrumptious puddings and jellies.

* Read more about starches on page 102.

1   Peel the cassava.

2   Grate the root.

3   Squeeze to remove the toxic juice.

4   Cook the starch to make tapioca flour.

ALL EYES ON ME

▸ The banks of the Amazon River ⑧ feature an incredible array of plants, including eye-catching **guaraná** ⑨.

▸ Guaraná fruits contain a large amount of caffeine. Resembling a cluster of eyes, their appearance is also quite eye-opening!

▸ What's more, legend has it that the first guaraná plant came about when a local god planted the eye of a dead child in the ground.

* See more about coffee and caffeine on page 107.

BERRY TERRIFYING

▸ According to legend, an ancient Amazonian tribe didn't have enough food, so their leader declared that all babies would have to be sacrificed to the gods. When the leader's daughter, Iaçá, gave birth to a son, he insisted that the baby be killed. Afterwards, she cried all night long. She was sure she could see her child at the foot of a tree but when she tried to put her arms around him, he disappeared. She was so devastated that she too died at the foot of the tree.

▸ The tribe discovered that the palm tree was covered in bunches of violet berries ⑦. These fruits allowed the tribe to survive, and the tree was named after Iaçá but spelt backwards, so acai.

▸ Acai berries are still popular today, and are often served as a delicious frozen mousse ④ ⑫.

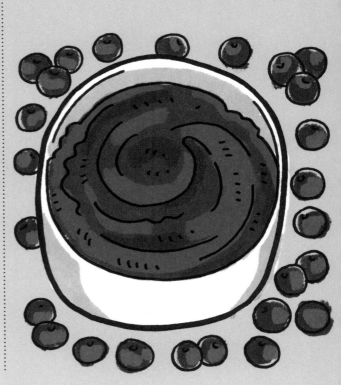

ARGENTINA
CATTLE COUNTRY

- The Pampas of Argentina are the country's most precious natural resource: these green, fertile plains provide the ideal conditions for raising livestock and developing agriculture.
- Before the Spanish conquistadors arrived 500 years ago, Argentina was made up of hunters and gatherers who lived simple lives.
- One of the first Europeans to make it to Argentina was Juan Díaz de Solís from Spain. His stories brought in the next wave of explorers in pursuit of the legendary hills of silver. The imaginary hills weren't found but the country was named after the precious metal anyway (*argentum* is the Latin word for silver).
- The native inhabitants were brutally defeated by the Spanish invaders and as a result, their culture and traditions were nearly wiped out.
- Once Argentina gained its independence from Spain, it became one of the wealthiest nations in the world — mainly thanks to its cattle rearing.

CARBONADA CRIOLLA
Beef and vegetable stew with fruit
🕐 1 hour, 5×🍲

 1 onion   2 garlic cloves   6 tbsp olive oil    600 g boneless beef

 3 tomatoes (400 g) or 1 can   2 laurel leaves   1½ cups beef broth (375 mL) or water

 2 small potatoes   2 small carrots   1 sweet potato   1 courgette

 1 peach   1 pear   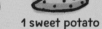 1 cob of corn or 1 cup frozen corn

 a handful of dried apricots   1 tsp oregano   1 tsp sweet pepper

 1 tsp thyme   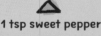 salt and pepper

1 Chop the onion and garlic and fry for several minutes on a medium heat, until soft.

MATAMBRE ⑩

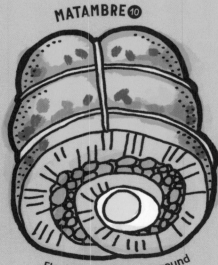

Flank steak wrapped around vegetables and a boiled egg.

EMPANADAS ⑪
Spanish-inspired deep-fried pastries, both sweet and savoury.

CARBONADA CRIOLLA ⑨

Beef stew with vegetables
(See recipe on the right-hand page).

Franco's whole family love his carbonada.

MEAT LOVERS' DREAM
- For centuries, great herds of cows have been grazing across the vast Pampas of Argentina. As cattle were mainly raised for their hides, there was an excess of meat. The local people needed to find new ways to preserve the meat before it spoiled.
- Some of the meat was made into jerky, (from the local Quechuan word Ch'arki), but before the invention of refrigerators, it was not possible to preserve or transport the meat in time.
- Even today, the average Argentinian consumes about 55 kg of beef (and nearly 100 kg of meat in total) every year.

2 Chop the meat into cubes and add to the pot. Add salt and fry until the meat is browned.

3 Cut the tomatoes into chunks (or use a can of chopped tomatoes). Add to the meat along with the laurel leaves and broth. Cover with a lid and cook for 30 minutes.

4 Peel the vegetables and fruit and cut into chunks.

5 Add the potatoes and carrots and cook for 10 minutes, then add the sweet potatoes. Stir and make sure all the ingredients are covered by the stock (if not, add more broth or water).

6 Add the courgette and corn. Cook for 10 more minutes or until all the ingredients are soft.

7 Add the fruit and spices and season.

BLUE SKIES FOR MILES
- **Gauchos** ❺❻❼ were local cowboys who today are a legendary symbol of Argentina. They spent their lives following herds across the Pampas and showing off their horse-riding skills.
- The gaucho's diet was simple: a serving of meat, followed by a second helping of meat. There were no vegetables in sight. The only distraction from an empty belly was a cup of brewed yerba mate (a type of herbal tea), that was meant to last the entire day.
- Today, gauchos are just a legend, but their meat-based diet still has an influence on Argentine cuisine.

SAVOURY SNACKS
- **Ch'arki** ❺ is the original Quechan word that was later adapted into English as 'jerky'.
- Salting and drying meat is a long-standing tradition across the Americas. The technique was used for all types of meat including beef. The meat was cut into thin strips, which was then salted generously and dried in the open air. Thanks to this process, the meat was preserved and could be stored for months at any temperature — and could also be eaten without cooking.

ASADO ACTION

▸ The gauchos didn't have anywhere to store provisions or pots and pans, so cooking was a challenge, but they did have easy access to beef.

▸ This is how the **asado** 4 8 method of cooking became popular. It means to roast over an open fire. The gauchos would use a bit of fencing or any type of metal frame to hold up the meat as it cooked.

▸ Today, the word *asado* not only refers to the traditional way of cooking meat, but also the festive social gathering around the fire pit.

Justus von Liebig

LANDY OF PLENTY

▸ 200 years ago, the people of Argentina had more meat available than they could possibly consume.

▸ The German chemist **Justus von Leibig** therefore produced a highly concentrated meat stock — a bit like a stock cube. It livened up soups and sauces and supplemented the diets of those who couldn't afford fresh meat.

▸ Producing these cubes in Europe was expensive, so Liebig started a company that used the overstock of beef in South America, making the product cheaper and more accessible.

IN THE TIME BEFORE CATTLE

▸ Before European cows arrived in Argentina, many other types of livestock were part of the local diet.

GUANACO
A mammal related to the llama*.
* Read more about llamas on page 44.

The rhea, or ñandú, is a cousin of the ostrich and emu. They eagerly gobble up locusts and other pests, but they also annoy farmers by digging up cabbage patches!

GREATER RHEA

DARWIN'S RHEA

fresh yerba mate leaves

dried and pulverised

bombilla

Special sieve for straining

Round gourd bowl

GREEN AWAKENING

▸ **Yerba mate ①** (mate tea) is the national drink of Argentina. It's made from leaves of the South American holly tree.

▸ The infusion is served in small, wooden cups or a special gourd bowl. The dried leaves are brewed with hot (not boiling) water and the tea can be sipped all day long through a bombilla — a metal straw.

▸ It has a high caffeine* content but, for a long time, was also considered a medicinal herb.

* Read more about caffeine on page 107.

CHOCOTORTA

Layered chocolate cake ⏱ 30 minutes, 8×🍰

1 can dulce de leche (510 g)

400 g cream cheese

¾ cup milk (190 ml)

400 g chocolate tea biscuits

½ cup double cream (125 ml)

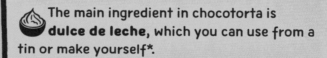
1 bar of dark chocolate (100 g)

🌀 The main ingredient in chocotorta is **dulce de leche**, which you can use from a tin or make yourself*.

1 In a bowl, combine the dulce de leche with the cream cheese. Pour the milk into a separate bowl. Prepare a rectangular tin.

2 Briefly soak each biscuit in milk and then arrange on the bottom of the tin. Add a layer of the dulce de leche mixture and then another layer of biscuits. Repeat until you have run out of biscuits ensuring there is a layer of dulce de leche on top.

* Find out how on page 46 (but double the ingredients).

Camila would like to eat chocotorta every day!

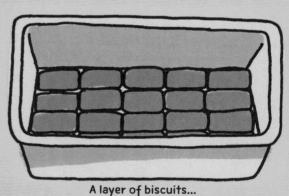
A layer of biscuits...

followed by a layer of dulce de leche mixture...

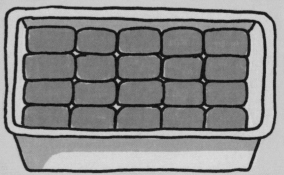
and so on...

3 Heat the cream in a pan. Break up the chocolate and add to the cream. Mix until smooth. Pour over the biscuits and set in the fridge for at least one hour.

NORWAY
WINTER IS COMING

Leif Eriksson

> This country in the very north of Europe is perfect for people who love nature and don't mind the cold.
> Norway's landscape is shaped by a glacier, which created its massive mountain ranges thousands of years ago. It also has a sprinkling of islands along the coast and its famous fjords ② are easily seen from the deck of nearby ships ⑬. Explorers willing to head further north can experience the midnight sun or polar nights!
> Visitors to Norway can witness the most fascinating of all natural phenomena on Earth — the aurora borealis, or northern lights ⑪.
> Living in such harsh conditions hasn't always been easy. There is little room for animals to graze between Norway's huge mountains and the long winters require a lot of food reserves.
> A popular way to tackle winter hunger was to preserve fish by fermenting, salting, smoking or drying. Moose ⑦, reindeer ④ and hares ⑥ were hunted ⑧, and Norwegians have a special way of baking thin, crispy bread ⑮.
> These tough conditions meant the Vikings were ruthless ①. Thanks to their long-lasting foodstuffs, they were able to sail to the furthest reaches of Europe — and even to North America.
> Norway's vast oil and gas supply ⑫ means they are one of the wealthiest countries in the world.
> Norwegians have however kept many elements of their traditional diet.

The salmon we eat today is mostly farmed ⑩. The fish have little room to move around so their meat ends up with fatty strips of white, and being kept in a confined space increases the risk of illness and parasites. Scientists are therefore trying to find more ecological solutions than farming.

Young salmon in the river

Adult salmon in the sea

Male salmon returning to the river

Female salmon returning to the river

CHANGELINGS
> Most fish can be classified by the water they live in — freshwater fish live in rivers and lakes and saltwater fish live in oceans and seas. The exception is salmon ③ ⑤ — which can live in both environments. They hatch from eggs at the bottom of a river and spend 2-3 years there before swimming along the current to reach the sea.
> After a few years at sea, salmon head back home. They swim upstream, against a vicious current. They change their appearance again and begin their spawning season. The females lay eggs and the males fertilise them. Sadly they die of exhaustion, but their eggs hatch and the lifecycle begins again.

NO EXPIRATION

▸ Fish are not the only food that can be preserved. The meat of domesticated cows ⑰, sheep ⑭ and pigs, as well as wild reindeer ④ and moose ⑦ can be salted, dried, and even smoked.

▸ Thanks to these traditional methods, these meats take on a richer flavour and last longer. They can then be enjoyed as cold cuts or added as an ingredient to cooked dishes.

SMALAHOVE

'Smale' means sheep and 'hovud' means head.

This traditional dish includes a sheep's head that has been salt-cured, smoked and steamed, served alongside potatoes and swede.

GENTLE FERMENTATION

▸ One of the earliest methods used to preserve salmon was to ferment the fish inside a pit dug on the seashore. Lactic acid-producing bacteria prevented the salmon from deteriorating, and gave it a distinct, sour taste.

▸ This is how **gravlax** is produced — the name literally means 'buried salmon'.

▸ Today, gravlax is made by marinating the salmon in lots of salt, sugar and dill, and then sealing it in a container for several days.

KJØTTKAKER MED BRUN SAUS

Meatballs in brown sauce
⏱ 45 minutes, 14×●

·········· Meatballs ··········

300 g ground beef	300 g ground pork	1 tbsp potato flour
⅓ tsp ground ginger		⅓ tsp ground nutmeg
3 tbsp milk	1½ tsp salt	pepper	butter (for frying)

·········· Brown sauce ··········

60 g butter	⅓ cups flour (60 g)	3 cups beef stock (750 ml)	salt and pepper

1 Combine the meatball ingredients by hand. Shape them into balls the size of a walnut. Melt 2-3 tablespoons of butter in a pan and fry the meatballs until browned.

2 For the sauce, first melt the butter in a pan. Gradually add the flour, whisking until the mixture is smooth. Reduce the heat and cook for 10 minutes, stirring from time to time.

3 When the sauce is browned, add the hot beef stock. Heat for another 10 minutes, until thick.

4 Season the sauce to taste and add the meatballs. Cover with a lid and cook for 15 minutes. Serve with potatoes.

TURBO FERMENTING

▸ For more intense flavour, or longer-lasting produce, fish can be fermented for several months, and even a year!

▸ Fermenting fish for this long produces the very pungent **rakfish**, meaning 'soaked fish'.

Bjørn is a big fan of kjøttkaker.

TOUGH CATCH

▸ For centuries, the most popular food in Norway has been tørrfisk (also known as stockfish) — cod that has been dried in cold air ⑨ until it is nearly as hard as a stone.

▸ Preserved in this way, tørrfisk keeps its flavour, can easily be transported and has a shelf life of many years. The only downside is that it must be soaked for a while before it can be cooked and served.

In the Middle Ages, Catholics did not eat meat during Lent. Stockfish was an easy substitution, and the rest of Europe soon joined the tørrfisk trend.

KILLER SAUCE

▸ Once it is properly soaked and cooked, stockfish can be eaten just like any other fish. Some connoisseurs go a step further and make **lutefisk** — 'dried fish soaked in lye'.

▸ Lye is highly toxic, but the dried fish soaks it in, swells and becomes very tender. The lye then has to be thoroughly rinsed off before cooking.

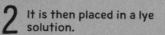

1. The stockfish is soaked in water for several days.

2. It is then placed in a lye solution.

3. It is then soaked in water again to get rid of the lye.

4. The fish is finally boiled and ready to eat.

DAIRY SUSTENANCE

▸ Norwegians also love cheese. One of the most popular types is called **brunost** ⑯, which simply means 'brown cheese'. Its colour and sweetish taste come from the heating process, which caramelises the sugar in the whey.

▸ The first person to produce brunost was **Anne Hov**, who came from Gudbrandsdalen. Her cheeses were a hit and soon other dairy farmers picked up on her method — which gave the local people a way to earn money.

ALWAYS TOGETHER

▸ The stars of Norwegian cuisine are not just salmon and cod — all sorts of fish are eaten every day.

SARDINE

These small fish travel in enormous shoals. Once they are caught, they are typically preserved in oil or marinade and canned.

HERRING

Much like sardines, herrings swim together. For hundreds of years, they were the most popular fish in Europe.

MACKEREL

A larger, migratory fast-moving fish.

The wavy lines on a mackerel's body help it to easily see the movements of the rest of shoal and change direction.

A SALTY ATTITUDE

▸ Water-loving microbes reproduce in moist food and cause it to spoil. However, if food is covered in salt (or immersed in a salty solution called brine), then through the process of **osmosis**, the salt will spread out, move to the surface and then evaporate.

▸ When foods are salted and dried, this hampers the reproduction of harmful microbes. At the same time, organisms responsible for fermentation continue to work and produce substances that are further toxic to unwanted bacteria. This entire process is behind the particular texture and flavour of gravlax.

* More on page 57.

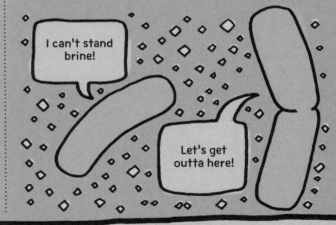

I can't stand brine!

Let's get outta here!

TILSLØRTE BONDEPIKER

Layered apple trifle
⏱ 30 minutes, 4×🥛

🍎🍎🍎
3 apples

🥛 ¼ cup water (60 ml)

△ 4 tbsp sugar (optional)

🍞🍞🍞🍞🍞🍞
6 slices crisp bread

🧈 50 g butter

△ ¼ tsp cinnamon

🥛 1 cup double cream (250 ml)

△ 2 tbsp powdered sugar

🍎 Most varieties of apples are sweet enough that they don't need any added sugar.

1 Peel and core the apples, cut into chunks and place into a pot with the water and half the sugar (if desired). Cook on a low heat until the apples turn mushy. Set aside to cool.

2 Blend the crisp bread in a blender. Melt the butter with the rest of the sugar then add the breadcrumbs and toast for a few minutes, stirring constantly. Add the cinnamon and cool.

3 Whip the cream with the powdered sugar until fluffy.

4 Fill a jar or glass with layers of apple, whipped cream and breadcrumbs.

A terrific trifle!

GERMANY

LAND OF SPÄTZLE, SAUSAGES AND WHITE GOLD

▶ Over time, German cooking became known as simple but filling. Tradition called for a big breakfast, a hearty lunch of noodles and schnitzels, an equally nourishing snack and, finally, a generous supper with all the family. The descendants of the ancient Germanic warriors didn't like getting up from the table until their bellies were properly full!

▶ So, while a solid serving of calories was the goal of German cuisine overall, the meals were still delicious and nutritionally balanced. Germany was once divided up between various nations and kingdoms, so every region has its own specialties.

▶ Beyond noodles, sausages, potatoes ❼❶❻❶⑲, sauerkraut❿ and rye bread, the region of Lower Saxony on the coast of the North Sea is known for its tasty fish dishes⓲.

▶ Global culinary trends have also made their mark on Germany in recent decades. Diners can now enjoy food from all over the world while Berlin has made a name for itself as the capital of modern German cuisine. Coveted Michelin stars* are now sprinkled throughout the land.

*Read more about Michelin stars on page 80.

OODLES OF NOODLES

▶ From **noodles** to all varieties of **dumplings**, Germans love pasta. It comes in all shapes, sizes and varieties. For example, dumplings can be made with flour, bread or potatoes, stuffed with fillings or drizzled in gravy. These doughy specialities can hold their own as a main dish or as a side.

BAVARIAN DUMPLINGS ❾

These are shaped from soaked breadcrumbs and filled with bacon, egg or cheese.

FRUIT-FILLED DUMPLINGS ❷

These generous packets are made potato flour and stuffed with plu strawberries❸, or blueberries.

NOCKERL ⓬
Originally from Austria, these noodles are made from a runny dough made of wheat flour that is dropped into boiling water on a spoon.

SPÄTZLE ⑮

These egg noodles are a perfect pairing for stews and sauces. Recipes include a smattering of onion and cheese (käsespätzle*) or stewed cherries and cinnamon (kirschspätzle).

*Recipe below.

DAMPFNUDEL ⓫

A yeasty dumpling boiled in milk and butter, served with meat or as a dessert.

KARTOFFELKLÖSSE ⓭

Plump potato dumplings.

KÄSESPÄTZLE

Cheesey drop noodles ⏱ 1 hour. 4× 🥣

 2¼ cups flour (340 g)

 ½ cup water (125 ml)

 4 eggs

 2 large onions

 4 tbsp butter (60 g)

 200 g cheese (that's good for melting: Emmental or Gruyère)

 bunch of spring onions

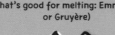 salt and pepper

1 Combine the flour, eggs, salt and water in a bowl. Continue mixing until you get a smooth, thick dough.

2 Bring a large pan of salted water to a boil. Dip a chopping board into the water, then spread a thin layer of dough

TOUGH CONTENDER

▶ Rye is a grain related to barley and wheat*. In the Middle Ages, it dominated when it came to bread, particularly in Central and Eastern Europe.

▶ This is because wheat grows well in the warmer regions of the south, whereas rye is more resilient to the harsh conditions of the north.

▶ Although wheat is now readily available, people still go wild for rye. The German black bread known as **pumpernickel**⑥ is baked at a low temperature for several hours to bring out rye's dense texture and sweetish flavour.

* Read about wheat on page 6.

I bought us each a loaf!

TOXIC TRANCE

▶ Medieval chronicles describe strange party scenes where a group of people would begin to dance, with some of them falling into a fever, with aches and chills.

▶ These unexpected events were caused by a fungus called ergot, which would attack crops of rye. Anyone who ate it would soon experience the strange symptoms of 'ergotism'.

▶ Luckily, we have ways to combat this fungus today.

3 When the noodles rise to the top, boil for a few more minutes, then drain and rinse.

4 Slice the onion thinly and fry in butter for 15 minutes, until golden. Grate the cheese and chop the spring onions.

5 Add the noodles to the pan of onions. Cook for a few minutes, then add the cheese and season. Sprinkle with spring onions and serve.

across it. Use a knife to cut the dough into noodles and drop them into the pan of boiling water.

Hannah's a fan of Käsespätzle.

TODAY'S BERLIN IS A WILD COCKTAIL OF FLAVOURS FROM ALL OVER THE WORLD

IT'S THE WURST!

▸ People have always taken care not to let meat go to waste. One of the oldest methods for using every part of an animal (trimmings, tripe, blood) is making **sausages ❶**.

▸ Meat is chopped or ground and then pushed into a casing (traditionally made from cow or pig intestines) and tied at the ends. Raw sausages can be boiled, roasted, dried or smoked.

▸ In Europe, sausages are usually made of pork, although plant-based fillings are now popular.

▸ Germans love **wurst**! There are over 1,500 different types, which can be divided up into three main categories based on how they are prepared.

BRÜHWURST
These sausages are boiled and then sometimes smoked. They can be eaten cold, but are usually heated.

FRANKFURTER
The type of sausage used for the American-style hot dog (see page 38).

WEISSWURST
A type of white sausage invented about 150 years ago. Because it spoils quickly, it was prepared in the morning and eaten for breakfast.

ROHWURST
Raw sausages that are dried and sometimes smoked.

TEEWURST
A spread made of finely-ground meat that can be used in sandwiches.

BRATWURST ❽
A famous grilled sausage with dozens of different varieties.

KOCHWURST
Cooked sausages that may be eaten cold.

LEBERWURST ❺
A sausage made with liver pâté.

BLUTWURST ⓮
These are filled with meat, fat and blood.

CURRYWURST
A fried bratwurst drizzled in ketchup and curry sauce.

This street food* hit was invented by wurst seller Herta Charlotte Heuwer.

* See more on street food on page 43.

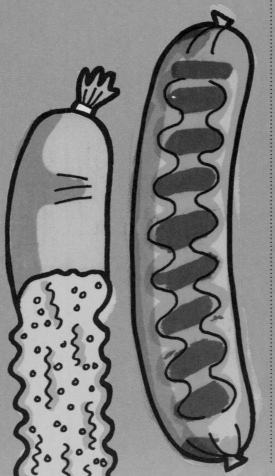

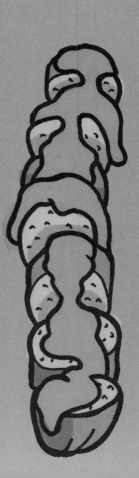

SPECTACULAR STALKS

▸ **Asparagus** ❹ ⑰ are the young shoots of a plant native to the Mediterranean basin. They were adored by the Romans. Emperor Augustus* was said to have had regular shipments of these green goodies.

▸ Each year, Germans eat 125,000 tons of white asparagus. For the two months they are in season, their consumption is an event of national proportions!

* Read more about Emperor Augustus on pages 89 and 98.

White and green asparagus are the same plant. The white variety is protected from the sun while growing. This stops it producing chlorophyll – the chemical which gives plants their green colour.

KARTOFFELSALAT

Potato salad ⏱ 45 minutes, 3×🍲

- 1 kg potatoes
- 1 cup beef stock (250 ml)
- 1 small onion
- 3 tbsp white wine vinegar
- 4–5 tbsp vegetable oil
- 1–2 tbsp mustard
- ¼ tsp nutmeg
- salt and pepper

·········· **Toppings** ··········

- fresh parsley
- 150 g bacon
- 2–3 pickles

Use whatever toppings you like!

1 Boil the potatoes in salted water until they are soft enough to poke with a fork. They should still hold their shape when cut. Drain and set aside to cool.

2 Heat the beef stock.

3 Dice the onion and add it to the stock. Cook on a low heat for a few more minutes.

4 Peel the potatoes into ½ cm thick slices. Pour the beef stock and onion over them, then add the vinegar, oil, mustard and nutmeg. Gently combine the ingredients and season. Set aside so the potatoes can absorb the dressing.

5 Add your selected toppings to the salad.

Leon has a side of Kartoffelsalat with every meal.

POLAND
FUNGI AND PICKLES

CASTLE AT OSTRÓW LEDNICKI

▶ Since the first king of Poland, Mieszko I ❷, took the throne, the borders of Poland have shifted. Four centuries ago, the Polish–Lithuanian Commonwealth was among the largest countries in Europe but it was eventually divided up during the 18th century. Poland didn't regain its independence until a century ago.

▶ Traditional Polish cuisine is known for its savoury, sour and herby flavours, its rich and fatty meats, and fish and venison (such as deer and boar) ❸. New influences were also brought in from Russia, Lithuania, Armenia, France, Austria and Germany, as well as Jewish people from all over Europe and the Middle East. The customary cabbage, beetroot and pickles were joined by potatoes, tomatoes, spinach, green beans, asparagus, cauliflower, courgette, lettuce, endives and leeks.

▶ The traditional Polish menu stuck fast to its typical kashas ❼ ⓫, breads ⓭, pierogis (Polish-style dumplings) ❹ ⓬, cheeses and other dairy products. Pork and poultry are as popular as ever, along with mushrooms ❻ ❾. A Polish dinner table is not complete without various types of fish ❶ ㉓, pickled vegetables ❽ ❿ and seasonal fruits.

MORE THAN MEAT AND POTATOES

▶ **Kasza** (kasha) refers to any variety of grain dish. These dishes date back thousands of years, and those who could afford it would enjoy kasha boiled with milk and eggs, and raisins or cinnamon ⓫. Others made do with a simple soup-like meal of kasha boiled in water.

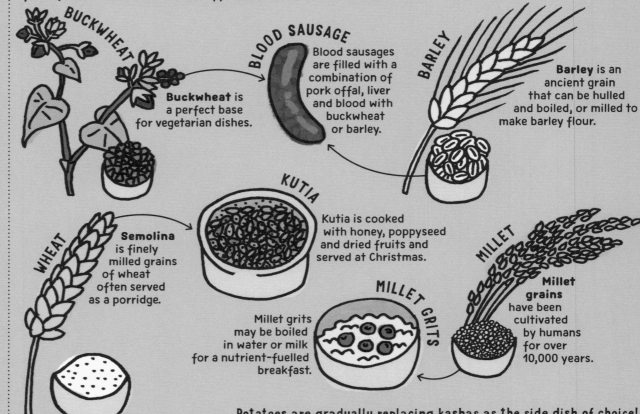

BUCKWHEAT

Buckwheat is a perfect base for vegetarian dishes.

BLOOD SAUSAGE

Blood sausages are filled with a combination of pork offal, liver and blood with buckwheat or barley.

BARLEY

Barley is an ancient grain that can be hulled and boiled, or milled to make barley flour.

WHEAT

Semolina is finely milled grains of wheat often served as a porridge.

KUTIA

Kutia is cooked with honey, poppyseed and dried fruits and served at Christmas.

MILLET

Millet grains have been cultivated by humans for over 10,000 years.

MILLET GRITS

Millet grits may be boiled in water or milk for a nutrient-fuelled breakfast.

Potatoes are gradually replacing kashas as the side dish of choice!

BUCKWHEAT AND CHEESE PIEROGI

Stuffed dumplings

⏱ 1 hour 15 minutes, 50× 🥟

Pierogis are the most recognisable of all Polish foods. Quite simply, they are wheat flour dumplings filled with sweet or savoury fillings.

1 Cook the buckwheat and set aside to cool. Add the cheese and mix well. Season to taste.

──── Filling ────

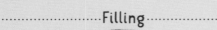
1 cup buckwheat (200 g)

500 g soft farmer's cheese

salt and pepper

──── Dumpling dough ────

3¼ cups flour (500 g) (plus a bit more for dusting)

1 egg

¼ tsp salt

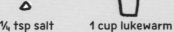
1 cup lukewarm water (250 ml)

serve with fried onion, sour cream

Natalia's pierogis are as big as grapefruits!

WILANÓW PALACE
IN WARSAW

John III Sobieski

Maria Kazimiera d'Arquien

PICKLE PARTY

▸ Pickling is one of the oldest methods of preserving food. This process is called **fermentation** and is made possible by the power of lactic acid bacteria.

PICKLED CABBAGE ⑧

SOUR CABBAGE STEW ⑤

Pickled cabbage (sauerkraut), meat and mushrooms stewed for several days.

PICKLED CUCUMBERS ⑩

PICKLE SOUP

SOUR SOUPS

▸ A proper Polish meal always starts with a bowl of soup and Poland is famous for its sour soups, such as **borscht**.

SOUR RYE SOUP

Topped with sausage and egg this soup has a sour rye starter as its base.
* Read more about sourdough starters on page 97.

RED BORSCHT

Pickled beetroot soup

SORREL SOUP

A lemony soup served with egg and sour cream.

SOUR CABBAGE SOUP

Full of pickled cabbage and meat

BUTTERMILK AND CHEESE

▸ Another famous fermented food is, of course, made from dairy. Buttermilk is a popular fermented drink made from milk that has been soured by bacteria*.

▸ Gradually heating soured milk provides a layer of clotted cream which can be used to make farmer's cheese — an essential ingredient in many Polish recipes, such as cheesecakes and pierogis.

* Store-bought milk is usually pasteurised: heated so all the bacteria is killed. To make sour milk and cheeses from pasteurised milk, adding a bit of unpasteurised cream or sour milk can kick-start the fermentation process.

2 Combine the flour and salt. Heap into the centre to make a little mound, then press down in the middle to create a well. Crack an egg into it, then start mixing the dough, gradually adding warm water. Knead it into a ball and cover with plastic film to keep it from drying out.

3 Cut a slice of the dough and form a roll about 3 cm in diameter. Place on your chopping board and cut it into smaller 2 cm slices. Dust with flour, flatten with your palm and roll out into discs about 2 mm thick.

4 Place a teaspoon of filling into the centre of each disc and seal up, pressing firmly around the edges.

5 Boil a big pan of salted water. Add the pierogis in small batches of around 10. Swirl the water around with a spoon to make sure they don't stick together. When they rise to the top, boil for just a few more minutes.

6 Garnish and serve. They can be fried for an added crunch.

TATRA MOUNTAINS

FOREST FRUITS

► Woodlands have long been a source of foraged foods, including venison, fruits, nuts and mushrooms.

► Over the past 200 years, most wild woodland has been cut down and foraged foods are less popular now due to the preference for farmed produce. They are, however, still an important element in Polish cuisine, and many recipes make use of 'wild' ingredients.

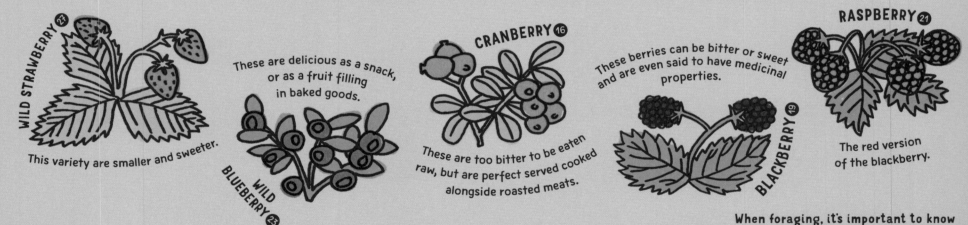

WILD STRAWBERRY 27
This variety are smaller and sweeter.

These are delicious as a snack, or as a fruit filling in baked goods.

WILD BLUEBERRY 23

CRANBERRY 16
These are too bitter to be eaten raw, but are perfect served cooked alongside roasted meats.

These berries can be bitter or sweet and are even said to have medicinal properties.

BLACKBERRY 19

RASPBERRY 21
The red version of the blackberry.

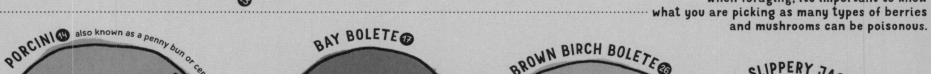

When foraging, it's important to know what you are picking as many types of berries and mushrooms can be poisonous.

PORCINI 14 also known as a penny bun or cep
A record-breaker, the biggest porcini ever found weighed in at a whopping 7.5 kg.

BAY BOLETE 17
This mushroom is poisonous if consumed raw, but cooking makes it edible.

BROWN BIRCH BOLETE 26
Its cap can be as broad as 20 cm, but the smaller mushrooms are tastier.

SLIPPERY JACK 25
The orange skin is bitter and can cause indigestion so should be removed.

PARASOL 22
This edible mushroom can easily be confused with the poisonous death cap, so care is needed when foraging.

SAFFRON MILKCAP 18
One of the most delicious fungi in the forest!

GOLDEN CHANTERELLE 20
These are perfect for sophisticated soups and sauces.

A NATIONAL SPORT

► Mushroom picking is a popular pastime in Poland. The season begins in August and goes through to late autumn. Every mushroom picker has their own preferred spots and species. Some families even take part in competitions! The winner of the latter category often scores quite a good souvenir photo to show off to all their friends 15.

Some varieties of edible mushroom can be grown on special farms, but many of the most valued species need to be tracked down in the forest's nooks and crannies.

MAZURY
LAKE DISTRICT

GOLD OF THE FOREST

▸ For hundreds of years before the advent of modern beekeeping, forest **beekeepers** would cut special holes in trees to draw out honey and beeswax from wild **hives**.

▸ The work of a forest beekeeper was difficult and dangerous because these hives were located high up in the tree. Their profession was highly respected.

▸ Today, the job no longer exists, although some modern beekeepers do sometimes take their hives into the forest for a short holiday 24.

Today, a single hive can produce up to 100 kg annually, compared to just a few kilograms per year in the past.

HONEY GINGERBREAD ⏱ 1 hour, chilling time: ⏱ 1 hour, 50×🌲

.... Cookie dough .... Icing ....

100 g honey	½ cup powdered sugar (65 g)	70 g butter	½ tsp baking soda	3 tbsp milk	egg white (1 egg)	1½ cup powdered sugar (195 g)

2 cups flour (300 g) (plus some extra for dusting)	pinch of salt	1 tbsp spice blend (ginger and cinnamon)	1 egg	1 tbsp lemon juice

Polish-style gingerbread is made with a generous dash of honey and spices.

1 Melt the butter, honey and powdered sugar in a pan. Mix the baking soda into the milk and add to the honey mixture. Stir well and cool.

2 Combine the flour, salt and spices. Heap the ingredients together to make a little mound, then press down in the centre to create a well. Add the honey blend and a whisked egg into the well. Mix the dough and knead, sprinkling with flour when necessary.

3 Form the dough into a ball, cover in plastic wrap and cool in the fridge for an hour.

4 Heat the oven to 180°C and cover a baking tray with wax paper.

5 Dust the chopping board with flour and roll the dough out until it is 3 mm thick. Cut out your favourite shapes using cutters, place on the baking tray, making sure to leave enough space between them. Bake each batch for 8–10 minutes.

6 Once your cookies are cool, it's time to decorate with icing! Combine the egg whites with the powdered sugar and lemon juice and blend until smooth. Make an icing bag by cutting a small hole in the corner of a plastic bag.

7 Store any leftover cookies in a jar.

Zosia is a master gingerbread maker!

RUSSIA
CAVIAR, TURNIPS AND ZAKUSKI

- Russia is the largest country in the world in terms of land mass. Spread over 17 million km², it is nearly twice as big as Europe!
- Historically, the Russian diet has been quite straightforward — the harsh winters and tough conditions meant survival was more important than cuisine.
- Filling foods like rye bread ❾, grain dishes (kasha), and root vegetables, which would eventually include potatoes (by the mid-19th century) were essential. Pickling was a popular method of preserving fresh foods, so the Russian palate grew fond of sour flavours. Their limited access to meat and other foods inspired hearty recipes for soups and stews ㉒ and the idea of making stuffed dumplings ⓭⓯ was eagerly adopted from China however, most of the spices and flavours from the east never really caught on here.
- Even today, the most popular Russian dishes are relatively simple in spite of their rustic origins and are as welcome in village huts as in the most palatial homes. Russian cuisine is appealing to labourers and emperors alike, from Ivan the Terrible to Peter the Great.

SMALL PLATES

- A traditional Russian feast involves different plates of warm and cold dishes, including cold cuts, pickled herrings, marinated or pickled vegetables and sandwiches. In Russian these small plates are known as 'zakuski' and are served as starters to a main meal or as a snack served over the course of a lengthy dinner.
- While Peter the Great may have developed his love of caviar from the lavish royal banquets of western Europe, the ingredients were always locally sourced.

BOILED DUMPLINGS ❼   PICKLES ⑱   JELLIED MEATS ⑯   BAKED DUMPLINGS ❽

SANDWICHES   CAVIAR ⑭   PICKLED HERRINGS ⑰   COLD CUTS ⑲

PICKLED CABBAGE ⑪   MARINATED MUSHROOMS ㉑   MARINATED VEGETABLES ⑳   HARD-BOILED EGGS

LUXURY FROM THE SEA

- Fish eggs are technically referred to as 'roe'. The roe produced by certain species of fish — in particular the sturgeon of the Caspian, Black and Azov Seas — is cured in salt to make **caviar** ⑭. This is by far the priciest of all zakuski.

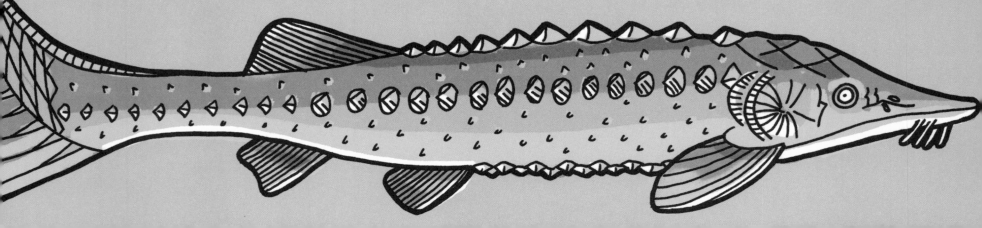

PELMENI PARADISE

▸ Dumplings have been a part of the Russian diet for hundreds of years. There are dozens of varieties of all different shapes and fillings ⑦ ⑬ ⑮.

▸ The most popular type of Russian dumpling is known as **pelmeni** — small pockets of dough that are filled with ground meat and served with cream and dill.

▸ Pelmeni originated in Siberia and the process of cooking and freezing meant meat could be preserved.

LITTLE SUNS

▸ Before Christianity was adopted by Russians about a thousand years ago, one of the most important holidays of the year was the Feast of Maslenitsa. Russians would say 'so long' to winter and 'hello' to spring with a party. The most popular dish was **blini** ⑫ — round yeasty pancakes made of buckwheat flour.

▸ Today, Maslenitsa is a Russian Orthodox holiday that is observed just before Lent. Blini are still popular and are enjoyed with sweet or savoury toppings.

Ikra is the Russian word for both fish roe and caviar. The English word 'caviar' comes from the Persian 'khâviyâr'.

BLINI
Buckwheat pancakes
For the dough: ⏱ 1 hour
Preparation: ⏱ 30 minutes, 15–20 🥞

½ cup wheat flour (65 g)	1 cup buckwheat flour (140 g)	½ tsp salt
2 tsp butter (30 g)	1¼ cups milk (320 g)	1 pack instant yeast (7 g)
¼ tsp powdered sugar	1 egg	vegetable oil for frying

········ Toppings ········

sour cream	fried onion	dill	smoked salmon

or anything you fancy!

1 In a large bowl, combine the flour and the salt. Melt the butter in a pan.

2 Gently warm the milk, add the yeast and powdered sugar. Mix, cover with a damp cloth and set aside for 10 minutes.

3 Add the melted butter, milk and egg yolk (save the white) to the dry ingredients. Mix thoroughly and leave the dough to rise for an hour.

4 Beat the egg white and add to the rest of the mixture.

5 Heat the oil in the frying pan. When hot, use a spoon to scoop small discs of the dough into the pan. Fry until golden on each side. Serve with your favourite toppings.

Sasha has whipped up a tower of blini for Anna.

LEGENDARY CLASSICS

▸ You might have heard of **kissel** before — a sweet sticky dessert made from stewed fruit juice.

▸ In the past, however, kissel was sour instead of sweet and made of fermented grain or boiled and whipped into a thick sauce.

▸ Legend has it that over 1,000 years ago, the residents of Belgorod survived an enemy occupation because of kissel.

KISSEL

Fruit dessert,
🕑 25 minutes, 4×🥛

🥛🥛🥛🥛
4 cups water (1 L)

500 g fresh or frozen fruits

△ 4 tbsp sugar (48 g)

△ 4 tbsp potato flour (100 g)
(or more, depending on desired thickness)

💧 ½ vanilla extract (optional)

1 Wash or thaw your fruits and add to a pan. Pour in 3 glasses of water and cook for 10 minutes until the fruit softens. Pass the mixture through a sieve to remove the pulp. Add sugar to the remaining fruit juice and heat until it has dissolved (add the vanilla here if desired).

2 Dissolve the potato flour in the remaining water then add to the fruit juice, stirring vigorously. Cook on a low heat for a few more minutes. If you want a thicker result, add a bit more flour (but remember to dissolve it first).

3 Pour the jelly into bowls or glasses and serve chilled.

Nastia loves super-thick jelly!

REFRESHING KVASS

▸ This sweet-and-sour fermented beverage ⑩ is made of rye* flour or a slice of toasted rye bread, sourdough starter or yeast, and some sugar.

▸ In the Middle Ages, everyone drank kvass — it's not as popular today, but you can still find it in Russian shops.

* Read more about rye on page 61.

1 Toast the bread.

2 Soak it in boiling water.

3 Drain in a sieve.

4 Add the sugar or honey, and yeast.

5 Allow to ferment.

6 It's ready to drink!

WINTER STORES

▶ Long and harsh winters have long been the bane of the average person's life in Russia. For centuries, hunger was chased away by **roots**, **bulbs** and **cabbage** — all nutritious and easy to store.

CABBAGE ❻
The first cabbage head (about 2,000 years ago) was just a tiny little ball, but this vegetable has grown over the years. It is an ideal food for fermentation ⓫, or can be boiled into a fine cabbage soup.

BEET ❺
The most popular type of beet is the round, crimson variety. However, its more common predecessor is long and yellowish in colour.

SWEDE ❷
The most subtle in flavour of all the roots, the suede is a cousin of the turnip and cabbage.

TURNIP ❸
Despite its plain appearance, this root vegetable has been key in feeding the rich and the poor across the world. In Russia, it was eaten at most meals — before it was pushed aside by the potato.

SUGAR BEET ❹
A quarter of all the sugar produced in the world today comes from sugar beets*. Karl Franz Archard opened the first sugar factory in Lower Silesia in 1801.

HORSERADISH ❶
Horseradish is part of the same family as cabbage. It is primarily used to add a dash of intensity to soups or dishes. As soon as you start grating the root, you can immediately feel the sharp twang in your nose and your eyes might start to water.

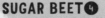
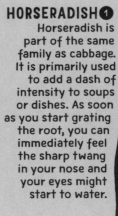
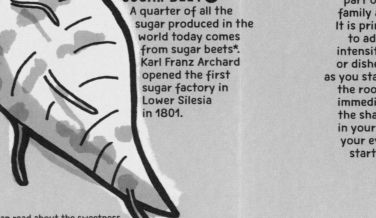

* You can read about the sweetness of sugar cane on page 27.

HUNGARY

FIERY PEPPERS ON HORSEBACK

▶ The ancestors of today's Hungarians came to Central Europe from the far reaches of Asia more than 1,000 years ago and settled on the vast steppes of the Pannonian Basin ①. In the year 1001, Stephen I became king of the newly established nation and introduced Christianity to his people.

▶ Agricultural practices sprang up quickly. The climate and the green valleys were ideal for raising horses ② and cattle ⑤. The entire steppe soon became one huge farm, but the Hungarian penchant for shepherding remained strong and the local cuisine was rich in meat and dairy.

▶ As Hungary grew in power, people travelled to settle there, adding their own influences to the local culture. Following a defeat in battle in 1526, the Turks ⑩ occupied the lands for the next 200 years and brought their own customs and specialities, including peppers ⑪, which were adopted into Hungarian cooking.

▶ Following years of hardship, Sultan Mustafa II ⑫ was defeated, and the German Habsburg dynasty ⑬ took over. Hungarians were now free to travel, trade and enjoy themselves ⑮; lavish banquets were held, and recipes were shared.

▶ As a result of the First World War, Hungary lost two thirds of its territory. Many of its people found themselves living in modern day Romania, Slovakia, Serbia, Ukraine and Austria. There are therefore, quite a lot of links between Hungarian cooking and many of the foods enjoyed in these countries.

LECSÓ

Tomato pepper stew
⏱ 50 minutes, 3× 🍲

1 tbsp lard
(or a few tbsp of veg)

2 medium onions

2 tbsp ground sweet or hot paprika
(or a blend of both)

4 differently coloured sweet peppers

1 tsp sugar

1½ tsp salt

3 medium tomatoes
(or 1 400g can)

250 g sausage
(optional)

pepper to taste

Great-grandfather András's own recipe

Grandfather Peter

Dad Tamás

Young Mr. László

1 If you are using fresh tomatoes, place them in boiling water and then remove the skins. Cut into large chunks. Cut the peppers and onions into thin strips.

2 Fry the onions until golden.

3 Add the paprika and continue cooking for another minute, stirring vigorously.

4 Add the chopped peppers, sugar and salt. Cook for 20 minutes until they are soft.

5 Add the tomatoes and sausage (optional). Cook for another 10–15 minutes, until some of the liquid has evaporated.

6 Season and serve with bread.

Goulash is a famous Hungarian stew. In Hungary, this dish is called pörkölt⓲.

STRAIGHT OUT OF THE POT

▸ Shepherds and cattle farmers used to graze their livestock on the Hungarian plains. The word **csikós** ❺ refers to a horse herdsperson*, while **gulyás** ❹ refers to a cattle herdsperson.

▸ At the Hortobagy National Park herdspeople still live their lives according to tradition. They're excellent riders and are often called 'Hungarian cowboys'.

▸ In the past, these herdspeople would never go anywhere without their clay (later copper or cast iron) pot for cooking classic Hungarian fish or meat stews ❽. Paprika became the seasoning of choice and breaded chunks of meat were tossed into hot lard, inspiring the name **pörkölt** ⓳, meaning to 'toast' or 'roast'. Meat stews are often served with sour cream ❼, potatoes or noodles ⓲.

* If you want to meet a csikós today, you would have to go to Hortobagy National Park, where these herdspeople still live their lives according to tradition. They're excellent riders as well, which is why they are often called 'Hungarian cowboys'.

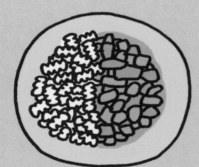

PÖRKÖLT   PAPRIKASH   GOULASH

Bogrács ❽ is the name of a special pot that is used to cook Hungarian stews.

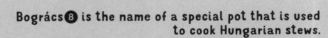

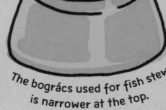

The bogrács used for fish stew is narrower at the top.

The bogrács used for meat stews is wider.

MOULDY MEATY TREATS

▸ True sausage* fans would find it hard to refuse a slice of Hungary's famous **téliszalámi** ❻ ⓴. Tradition states it should only be produced in winter and so it is also known as 'winter salami'.

▸ The salami is smoked and then put in cold storage for several months to dry, ferment and… get mouldy. And not just a little bit mouldy, it must be completely covered in a specific type of mould to keep toxic bacteria out and provide flavour.

* Hungarian sausages are not only made of meat: Hurka⓱ is made with rice and pig's blood or liver.

Téliszalámi was originally made from donkey meat, but it prompted a shortage of donkeys so mangalica ❾ was used instead – a furry cross between a pig and a boar.

Better you than me!

MEGGYLEVES

Sour cherry soup

⏱ 30 minutes, 4×🍲

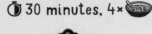

1 kg cherries
(freshly pitted or thawed with their juice)

6 cups water
(1½ L)

6 tbsp sugar

pinch of salt

4 cloves

lemon peel

cinnamon stick

1 cup thick cream
(250 ml)

1 tbsp flour

whipped cream
(for decorating, if desired)

🍒 Traditionally, meggyleves was made with whole cherries, but it's easier to eat if the cherries have been pitted.

🍲 Fruit stews are popular in the east and north of Europe. They can be served hot or cold, with a dollop of cream or milk.

If you don't have a cherry pitter, you can use a bottle and a straw...

... or a paperclip

Place the cherry at the top of the bottle

Using the straw, push the pit into the bottle.

0 ----> S

Shape the paper clip into the letter 'S'.

Push the clip into the cherry and hook the pit.

Remove the pi[t]

For centuries, it was believed that Columbus was the first to sail from Europe to the land that is now called America. However, it is likely that the Viking, Leif Eriksson, got there 500 years earlier.

See more about Eriksson on page 56.

THE CARIBBEAN

1 In 1492, Christopher Columbus travelled from Spain to the Caribbean and encountered the native population.

2 Columbus kidnapped the native people, stole their valuables and their produce (pineapples, turkeys and peppers) and travelled back to Spain.

SWEET AND PRETTY

▶ Peppers are a Hungarian's favourite vegetable. Tied up on a string and dried ⑭ or ground up into a fine powder, it is used in sausage ⑯,

soups, sauces and goulash ⑲. It gives dishes a distinctive paprika taste and rusty colour.

▶ Fresh paprika is eaten raw in salads or used in meat and vegetable* stews.

* See the recipe on page 72.

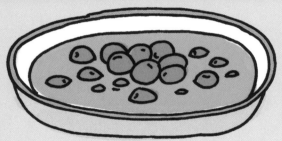

1 Put the cherries in a pan, add the water and bring to boil. Add the sugar, salt, cloves, lemon peel and cinnamon stick. Cook for 15 minutes.

2 Add a few tablespoons of the hot stew to the cream. Add the flour and mix thoroughly to get rid of any lumps.

3 Remove the cloves and lemon peel, add the cream mix and cook for a few more minutes.

4 When the stew has cooled, place it in the fridge. Serve it cold with a dollop of whipped cream.

Réka's son loves meggyleves!

3 Palace gardens and church properties were decorated with pepper plants.

EUROPE

THE BALKANS

SPAIN

4 Paprika made it to Africa and Asia via trade routes.

When the Turks invaded Hungary, they brought paprika ⑪ with them but to begin with the plants were used as a decoration.

5

6 At the start of the 19th century, paprika become Hungary's favourite spice — and it still is!

▶ For a long time, peppers were spicy — sweet peppers weren't cultivated until around 100 years ago.

▶ The Hungarian love for paprika is clear from the number of paprika festivals and museums in the country.

▶ Paprika plays a vital role in Hungarian cuisine, which is quite an achievement considering it has only been around for 200 years.

 AUSTRIA-HUNGARY

SPAIN SMALL PLEASURES

▶ The sunny cuisine of Spain has been shaped by thousands of years of tumultuous history. Some 2,500 years ago, the Phoenicians and Greeks brought over olives **1**. A few centuries later, the Romans began making wine **2**. The Germans arrived 600 years later and perfected beer-brewing techniques **3**.

▶ Arabs arrived in the 8th century bringing the culinary gifts of almonds, sugar cane, aubergines, watermelons, peaches, sesame and spices **4**.

▶ In the 15th century, Spain's new Christian rulers began their inquisition **5**. At the same time, Spanish explorers set off in search of new lands. Christopher Columbus[1] **6** brought new plants and spices back from the Caribbean, Hernán Cortes **7** obliterated the Aztecs and Francisco Pizarro **8** damaged the Incan empire[2]. Spanish cuisine spread to new lands, while also embracing new ingredients and flavours from across the Atlantic, such as potatoes and peppers.

[1] See more on Columbus on page 74.
[2] See more about the Aztecs and Incas on pages 40 & 44.

THE RIGHT MIX

▶ The Romans brought their metal pots to the Iberian peninsula while rice arrived with the Arabs about 900 years later. The combination of the two eventually led to **paella**, a dish initially enjoyed by farmers.

▶ The most popular version of this dish comes from Valencia and contains rice, saffron, meat, string beans and lima beans, snails, tomatoes and peppers.

▶ A huge paella pan filled with goodies is the most popular way to celebrate a special occasion in Spain.

The word 'paella' comes from the Latin word 'patella', meaning 'round pan'.

TORTILLA* DE PATATAS
Potato onion omelette
🕐 50 minutes, 4×🍽

900 g potatoes

1 onion

¾ cup olive oil (190 ml)
(or other vegetable oil)

1 tsp salt

8 eggs

Alejandro is very good at flipping!

1 Peel the potatoes and cut into thin slices. Dice the onions.

2 Add the oil to a frying pan about 25 cm in diameter. Add the potatoes, onion and salt.

3 Cover with a lid and fry for 20 minutes, or until the potatoes are soft. Stir occasionally.

4 Whisk the eggs. Strain the oil from the potatoes and onions and mix into the eggs.

* Not to be confused with Mexican corn tortillas (page 42).

FINGER FOODS

► The rocky cliffs off the Atlantic and Mediterranean are home to a peculiar creature that pokes out occasionally as it filters the seawater in search of nutrients.

► A type of crustacean, these creatures are called **percebes** ㉕ in Spanish and 'goose barnacles' in English, and happen to be among the most expensive delicacies in the world.

The part of the barnacle that is eaten is the muscle inside the tough outer skin.

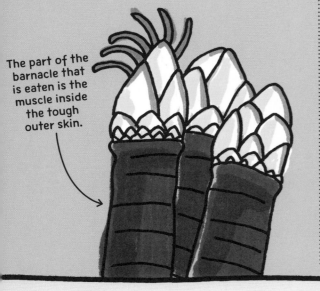

MISSION IMPOSSIBLE

► Fixed fast to sharp, rocky cliffs that are constantly battered by the waves, collecting these barnacles is dangerous and causes numerous accidents every year.

► This, coupled with the fact they are quite rare, explains why goose barnacles are so expensive. There are now limits on how many can be harvested to prevent a decline in numbers.

LUXURY SWINE

► Spain's famous **jamón serrano** (serrano ham) has been produced in the same way for over 2,000 years: pork meat is immersed in salt for two weeks, dried for six months and left to mature in the open air for another few months.

► **Jamón ibérico** ⑭ comes from the meat of black pigs that are said to be a crossbreed of white domestic pigs and wild boars. This 'wild' quality is said to give the ham its remarkable flavour.

5 Wipe the pan clean and heat up a few tablespoons of oil. Add the egg mixture and cook under a lid for 15 minutes.

6 When the edges of the tortilla are golden and the top is almost cooked, cover the pan with a large plate and flip the pan over. Slide the tortilla back into the pan and cook the other side for 5 minutes. You may need an adult to help with this.

IT'S GETTING HOT IN HERE...

▶ The best-known Andalusian specialities are cold soups known as **gazpachos** 🔟🏷, perfect for scorching hot summer days. They are made from raw vegetables and stale bread, seasoned with olive oil, vinegar and garlic*.

▶ This type of refreshment has been known to locals since the Middle Ages, but as tomatoes and peppers didn't arrive in Europe until much later, the classic recipe was based on bread, garlic, almonds, olives and vinegar. There is also a garlic-based version known as **ajoblanco** 🏷.

▶ The word 'gazpacho' now refers to any type of Spanish soup served cold.

* See the recipe below.

NO RUSH

▶ Eating on the go is sometimes the only option but there isn't much pleasure in rushing through a meal and ending up with indigestion!

▶ It's much nicer to take the time to enjoy a meal, especially if surrounded by friends.

▶ This laid-back approach to dining is known as **sobremesa** in Spain — and it's definitely a tradition that should be adopted by everyone.

ANDALUSIAN GAZPACHO 🏷

AJOBLANCO 🏷

SALMOREJO 🏷
This Cordoba-based recipe features tomatoes, garlic, olive oil and bread.

AVOCADO GAZPACHO 🏷

MELON GAZPACHO 🏷

WATERMELON GAZPACHO 🏷

GAZPACHO
Chilled tomato soup
Preparation: ⏱ 20 minutes
Chilling: ◉ 1 hour, 4 × 🍲

 100 g white bread slices

 1 kg ripe tomatoes

 ½ fresh cucumber

 1 pepper

 1 small onion

 1 clove garlic

 3–4 tbsp olive oil

 3 tbsp wine vinegar

salt and pepper

·········· Accompaniments ··········

 tomatoes

 pepper

 cucumber

hardboiled eggs

1 Cut the bread into small pieces, cover with a cup of water and leave to soak.

2 Blend together the tomatoes, cucumber, pepper, onion and garlic. Drain the water from the bread and add vegetable mixture, along with the olive oil and vinegar. Blend again and season to taste.

3 You can pass the gazpacho through a sieve to make it smoother. Serve chilled.

Sofia uses her grandmother's recipe.

A SINGLE BITE

▸ The best way to sample Spanish flavours in one go is by having **tapas**: warm and cold starters that are served on small plates.

▸ Tapas are quite popular in Spain, but this type of dish isn't cooked at home. Instead Spaniards go to tapas bars to enjoy a drink and a snack with friends.

▸ Wandering from bar to bar in pursuit of the perfect tapas is known as **tapeo**. It's a popular Spanish pastime and a great way to get to know new people.

JAMÓN IBÉRICO 14

ACEITUNAS 15
Plain or stuffed olives.

NAVAJAS 22
Fried razor clams.

POLBO Á FEIRA 24
Cooked octopus with paprika.

PERCEBES 25
Goose barnacles served raw or cooked.

CROQUETAS 27
Meat, fish, cheese or vegetables encased in bechamel sauce, breaded and fried.

TORTILLA DE PATATAS 30
A potato and onion omelette.

CARACOLES 18
Cooked snails.

BOTIFARRA 9
Catalan-style sausage.

CALAMARES 10
Sliced and fried calamari (squid).

HUEVOS ESTRELLADOS 16
Fried eggs, often served with ham.

PATATAS BRAVAS 20
Fried potatoes in a spicy sauce.

COJONUDO 28
Bread topped with chorizo and a fried egg.

PESCAÍTO FRITO 17
Lightly breaded and fried fish.

LA BOMBA 21
Deep-fried ground meat with a layer of potato and breadcrumbs.

BOQUERONES EN VINAGRE 11
Fresh anchovies in vinegar.

FRANCE
REVOLUTIONARY TASTES

Charles VI

Louis XIV

Madame de Pompadour

Louis XV

François Pierre de la Varenne

Guillaume Tirel

François Massialot

Vincent La Chapelle

▶ France — the name itself gives rise to so much fanciful imagery: snowy Alpine peaks, vast vineyards, medieval castles, illustrious palaces and enormous cathedrals. Then there's Paris, considered by many to be the cultural capital of Europe. French culture and its exquisite cuisine have long-inspired awe across the world.

▶ France has a temperate climate and a varied landscape, and the French have always made the most of their natural resources — the fruits of the fields, forests, mountains and seas.

▶ The French believe that food is meant to be a source of pleasure and this passion has fed the imaginations of the nation's chefs. These professionals have never been afraid to break with the past and face up to new culinary challenges.

▶ The rest of the world finally caught up with the French, however, and their legendary achievements continue to inspire each new generation of chefs.

Sous-chef

Sauce chef

Seafood chef

Soup chef

Baker

... and many more!

A GREAT TEAM
▶ The word 'chef' comes from the French 'chef de cuisine' — the person in charge of the menu, the dishes and the entire team of cooks.

▶ It's important each member of the kitchen team knows exactly what they are doing. The **brigade system** ❻ was devised by celebrated chef **Georges Auguste Escoffier** ❼ and gave each cook a specific task.

Three stars: worth travelling across the country for!

Two stars: worth taking a detour!

One star: worth making the trip!

BRIGHTEST STARS
▶ **Jean Anthelme** ❸ wrote witty essays about the joys of fine food two centuries ago. He founded the culture of culinary critiques and the practice of rating restaurants and their menus.

▶ The red Michelin* restaurant guide appeared on the scene about a century ago. Receiving even a single Michelin star is enough to make a restaurant famous.

* Michelin is the name of a French tyre producer. The company began publishing its food guide when cars were still a novelty. The goal was to encourage motorists to travel — the idea being, the more people who drove cars, the more often they'd need replacement tyres!

BÉCHAMEL ❷
A simple sauce made from butter, flour and whole milk.

TOMATO
Puréed tomatoes cooked with olives and onion.

VELOUTÉ
Light roux of butter, flour and stock.

HOLLANDAISE
Creamy sauce made from whipping together butter, lemon juice or wine and egg yolks

ESPAGNOLE
Rich, dark sauce made from roux-thickened stock, puréed tomatoes and vegetables.

GERMAN SAUCE
A velouté of egg yolks and cream that was rejected by Escoffier.

FLUID FOUNDATIONS
▶ There are hundreds of different sauces in French cuisine. Thankfully, there are four basic foundations from which they are all made, the rules having been devised by Marie-Antoine Carême ❹.

▶ A number of years later, the famed chef Georges Auguste Escoffier added two new sauces to the list — but rejected one — creating the now universal list of **five French mother sauces** ❺.

Napoleon I

Joséphine Bonaparte

Jean Anthelme Brillat-Savarin

Marie-Antoine Carême

Jules Gouffé

Henri-Paul Pellaprat

PASTRY TOWERS

▶ The portrait gallery of accomplished French chefs is full of illustrious characters including **Marie-Antoine Carême 4**.

▶ Carême was born into a poor family and, as a child, he found a job working at a restaurant.

▶ In time, Carême became an apprentice to Sylvain Bailly — a renowned French pastry chef. He also discovered a love of architecture that inspired his incredible towering desserts. He drew inspiration from famous buildings and monuments and came up with his own decorative style of serving various dishes.

▶ After years of hard work, he became a master of cuisine. He prepared glorious meals for many heads of state, including Napoleon and King George VI of the United Kingdom.

▶ Carême left behind a glittering legacy. Today, he is known as the creator of **haute cuisine**, or 'high cuisine', which raises everyday cooking to the highest level of refinement. The technique, ingredients and the manner of serving each dish are all impeccable.

Maxime likes to add a double helping of cheese!

CROQUE MONSIEUR

Ham and cheese toastie 🕐 30 minutes, 5×🥪

········· Béchamel sauce ·········

1 cup milk (250 ml) · 40 g butter · 2 tbsp flour (20 g)

Pinch of nutmeg · salt · pinch of white pepper (optional)

140 g Gruyère · 10 slices of bread · 5 slices of ham · dollop of Dijon mustard

1 Prepare the béchamel sauce by warming the milk in one pan and melting the butter in another. Slowly add flour to the melted butter, whisking energetically. Heat for about a minute, until it starts to bubble.

2 Slowly add the warm milk, mixing the entire time. Cook on a low heat for another 5 minutes. Add the nutmeg, salt and pepper.

3 Heat the oven to 180°. Grate the cheese.

4 Toast the bread in the oven and spread a spoonful of béchamel sauce on each slice. Add a slice of ham, a bit of mustard, sprinkle with cheese and top with the other slice of bread. Cover in bechamel sauce and sprinkle with some more cheese.

5 Set each croque monsieur on a baking tray and bake for 7 minutes. Switch to the grill setting for the last 2 minutes so that it browns on top.

81

Marlene Dietrich – actress

Charles de Gaulle – French President

Valéry Giscard d'Estaing – French President

Anne-Aymone Giscard d'Estaing – French First Lady

Marie Bourgeois

Eugénie Brazier

Georges Auguste Escoffier

Paul Bocuse

MILLE-FEUILLE

Layered pastry dessert ❶

◉ 1 hour, 6× 🍰

------- Cream -------

🥛 1 cup milk (250 ml)

🫚 1 vanilla pod (or 1 tsp vanilla essence)

🥚🥚🥚🥚🥚 5 eggs

△ 2 tbsp sugar

△ 1 tbsp flour

△ 1 tbsp potato starch

🌀 300 g frozen French pastry dough

△ 2 tbsp powdered sugar (for sprinkling)

------- Decoration -------

△ 6 tbsp powdered sugar

💧 1 tbsp water

△ cocoa

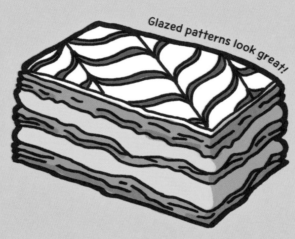

Glazed patterns look great!

! The day before you plan to bake, put the frozen pastry into the fridge.

1 Pour the milk into a pan. Add the vanilla beans and pod to the milk and heat. Separate the egg yolks from the whites. In a large bowl, combine the yolks with the sugar and the flour and starch, mixing thoroughly.

2 Take the vanilla pod out of the mixture and keep stirring as you pour the milk into the yolks. Then pour it all back into the pan and cook for several minutes, stirring constantly, until it is smooth and thick.

3 Cover the cream with cling film and set aside to cool.

4 Heat the oven to 200°C. Place the pastry dough on a flour-dusted surface. Cut into 18 even squares (they'll need to be cooked in two batches).

5 Cover a baking tray with baking paper. Arrange half the pastry squares, spear with a fork and dust with a pinch of powdered sugar. Cover with another sheet of baking paper, place another tray on top and press down (this will keep the pastry from rising). Bake for 15–20 minutes, until the squares are golden and flaky. Repeat for the second batch and allow to cool.

6 Cover 6 squares with cream, then cover 6 more squares with cream and place on top. Do this for a third layer.

7 Make a glaze from the powdered sugar mixed with water and top with cocoa. You can experiment with patterns.

Chloe bakes mille-feuille every first Saturday of the month and eats half of it herself!

THICK AND BUTTERY

▸ A **croissant** is a delicate crescent of flaky pastry and a symbol of a traditional French breakfast. There are many myths about how it came about, but the most contemporary version dates back to around a century ago. The croissant gets its fluffy texture from a special **laminating technique**, which consists of kneading and rolling layer after layer of dough and butter.

▸ As it bakes, the butter melts, leaving behind gaps that are filled with hot air. This is why the croissant puffs up.

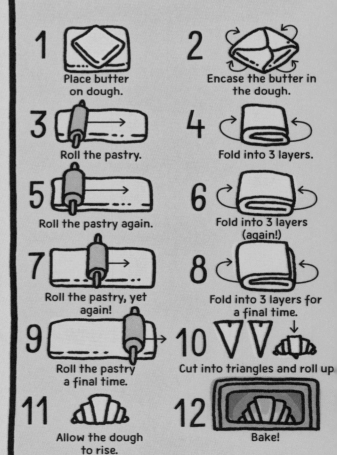

1 Place butter on dough.

2 Encase the butter in the dough.

3 Roll the pastry.

4 Fold into 3 layers.

5 Roll the pastry again.

6 Fold into 3 layers (again!)

7 Roll the pastry, yet again!

8 Fold into 3 layers for a final time.

9 Roll the pastry a final time.

10 Cut into triangles and roll up

11 Allow the dough to rise.

12 Bake!

Croissant pastry dough contains yeast. The butter makes it delightfully flaky, and rich too!

Charlene Grimaldi – Princess of Monaco

Albert II Grimaldi – Prince of Monaco

Alain Ducasse

Alain Passard

Anne-Sophie Pic

Hélène Darroze

Pierre Hermé

CHEESE PARADISE

▶ France is famous for its wonderful cheeses. Cheese is served with most meals and even as an actual course.

▶ The French make cheese from cow, sheep and goat's milk. It can be hard or soft, fresh or mature — in fact there is a different type of French cheese for every day of the year!

CAMEMBERT

A soft cheese with a delicate velvety rind. It's sold in wooden boxes to keep its shape.

ROQUEFORT

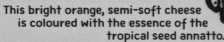

This blue cheese gets its colour from a harmless mould. It matures in the chalk caves near the town of Roquefort-sur-Soulzon.

MUNSTER

Soft cheese with an intense scent and slightly sharp flavour.

BRIE

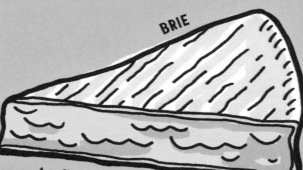

A soft, oozy cheese that has been enjoyed since the Middle Ages.

MIMOLETTE

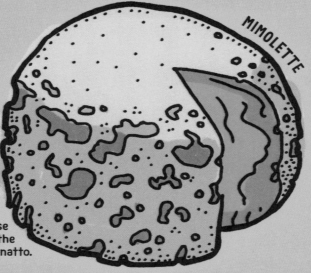

This bright orange, semi-soft cheese is coloured with the essence of the tropical seed annatto.

SIMPLE AND EFFECTIVE

▶ Milk is an ideal environment for microorganisms that cause illnesses or make food turn mouldy.

▶ **Pasteurisation** was developed by the French chemist Louis Pasteur and requires heating liquids to just under 100°C. His work led to a new field of science known as microbiology.

▶ The heating process halts the reproduction of microorganisms in foods without changing their nutritional content or flavour.

▶ Thanks to pasteurisation, milk stays fresh for longer and there's no risk of passing on diseases such as tuberculosis, or bacteria such as salmonella.

My milk has gone off!

Louis Pasteur

I must do something about it...

CURDLING ACTION

▶ One way to turn milk into curd (a base for cheese*) is to add rennet, a digestive enzyme.

▶ Rennet is required to make lots of different cheeses. It can be obtained from the stomach of a young calf and can also be found in certain plants, but the quickest way to get hold of it is to make it in a laboratory.

* Check out the secrets of cheesemaking on page 65.

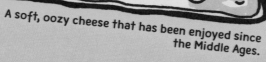

ITALY
INGREDIENTS ARE KEY

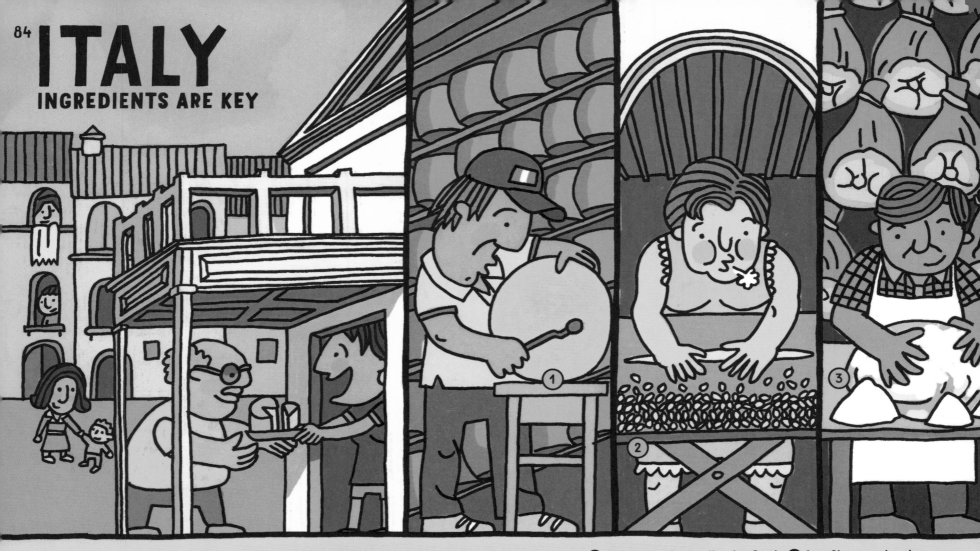

▶ The leaders of Ancient Rome first won the territory of modern-day Italy and then neighbouring regions, creating one of the most powerful regimes in history — the Roman Empire.

▶ When the empire finally collapsed, its territories were divided up into individual kingdoms, republics and cities, but Italy wasn't officially united until 1861.

▶ Italy is made up of 20 distinct regions, each with its own customs and traditions. The south is known for its tomatoes, fiery peppers, artichokes㉔ and aubergines. Fish and seafood⑲ are plentiful along the coast, and Sicily is famous for its juicy oranges and delicate wines. A national specialty is a rice dish known as risotto⑳ and polenta⑨. The region of Liguria is famous for making the most aromatic of olive oils㉓.

▶ In Italy, there is always a reason to celebrate. Italian cooking is relatively straightforward, but the key to its unique flavours is high quality ingredients. Pasta❷ is often made at home and its shape adapted to each type of sauce. The average Italian person eats about 27 kg of pasta each year! This can be boiled, baked, stuffed or layered, like lasagne㉑.

▶ Italian cuisine has become famous all over the globe. Pizza㉕ parlours are found in most cities, along with Italian restaurants and gelato⑫ shops. And who can resist a creamy tiramisu⑭?

▶ The great expansion of Italian cuisine continues.

TAGLIATELLE ALLA BOLOGNESE
Pasta with a tomato-meat sauce. Preparation: ⏱ 30 minutes, simmer: ⏱ 1 hour, 4× 🍝

Bolognese is a type of **ragù** (a slow-cooked, meat-based sauce) from the city of Bologna. While spaghetti is often associated with this dish, Italians believe a true Bolognese calls for tagliatelle!

 1 medium onion

  2 small carrots

 1 celery stalk

 70 g smoked bacon

 5–6 tbsp olive oil

 500 g ground beef

2 cups beef broth (500 ml)

 1 can chopped tomatoes (400 g)

 ½ cup milk (125 ml)

 3 tsp tomato paste

 500 g tagliatelle pasta

 parmigiano (parmesan) for garnish

 salt and pepper

1 Cut the onion, carrots, celery and bacon into small cubes. Take a deep pan and heat up a few tablespoons of oil. Add the vegetables and salt and fry for about 10 minutes, stirring occasionally.

UNDERGROUND ELITE

▶ One of the most remarkable and expensive delicacies in the world is the **truffle**⑩. Edible fungi* that grow underground, truffles can be enjoyed raw or cooked as part of a dish.

▶ It's extremely difficult to find truffles, which is why hunting for them is a popular sport. Pigs were once used to sniff them out, but today specially trained dogs are used⑥.

▶ Anyone who manages to find a truffle has a real treasure on their hands — a few kilograms of white truffle can possibly even fetch enough cash to buy a car!

* Read more about fungi on page 66.

There are about a dozen different truffles, but two are in high demand:

BLACK TRUFFLES
Gathered mainly in France, these are more common than the white variety.

WHITE TRUFFLES
The queen of all fungi, these are mainly gathered in the Piemonte region of Italy.

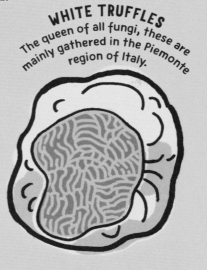

LEAFY SAUCE

▶ **Pesto** ⑦ is a wonderfully simple sauce made of basil. Its flavour depends on the quality of the individual ingredients. Simply mash everything together in a mortar, and then add to hot pasta!

▶ But do be careful! This simple recipe can't allow for any shortcuts or substitutions — limp basil just won't cut it!

BASIL

Take care not to cook your basil because it may turn bitter.

PARMIGIANO-REGGIANO

PECORINO SARDO

PINE NUTS

These little nuts are seeds from a pine cone but very few species of the tree produce big enough seeds to harvest.

OLIVE OIL

GARLIC

SALT

PESTO

2 Add the ground beef and bacon. Cook until the meat has browned.

3 Pour in a cup of broth and cook for a few minutes on a high heat, until half the liquid has evaporated.

Ms. Laila prefers to make her own tagliatelle from scratch.

4 Add the chopped tomatoes and puree. Cover and simmer on a low heat for 1–2 hours, stirring from time to time.

5 Midway through, add the second cup of broth. Add the milk at the end and cook for a few minutes. Season to taste.

6 Cook the tagliatelle according to the packet instructions and cover with sauce. Sprinkle with parmesan and pepper. Buon appetito!

PETALS OF DELIGHT

▶ According to legend, the Greek god Zeus fell in love with a mortal named Cynara. He made her a goddess and took her back to Mount Olympus. Cynara missed her family so returned home. Furious, Zeus turned her into an **artichoke** — a flower that is both beautiful and tasty, as long as it's eaten before it blooms.

To enjoy an artichoke, pluck off and eat the edible portion at the base. The heart of the artichoke is the tastiest bit of all.

The outer petals are not edible and must be discarded.

After the artichoke blooms, it is essentially inedible.

Artichokes can be boiled, fried, stuffed ㉔, baked or marinated.

FOR ANY OCCASION

▶ Italy has hundreds of regional cheeses and each one has its own unique character.

Some have even risen to the ranks of world-class status!

PARMIGIANO-REGGIANO ①

Made of cow's milk, this type of cheese has been produced for nearly 1,000 years. In English, we tend to call it 'parmesan' for short. It takes about 12 months to mature.

MOZZARELLA ㉒

A soft, squishy cheese from the milk of a cow, buffalo or even a goat. It is a key pizza ingredient.

MASCARPONE

Made from the thick, sweet cream skimmed from cow's milk, it is ideal for making creamy sauces and rich desserts — in particular tiramisu ⑭.

PECORINO ⑰

Sharper in flavour than its cousin Parmigiano-Reggiano, pecorino is made from sheep's milk.

GORGONZOLA ⑯

A classic blue cheese, mouldy bits form in holes drilled into the cheese during the ripening process. This adds to the intense flavour.

RICOTTA

A delicate cheese made from whey, which is the liquid left behind after separating the curd*, ricotta is used to make Italian pastries known as cannoli ⑧ ⑮.

* Find out more on page 83.

HAMMING IT UP

▶ Another Italian classic is **prosciutto crudo ③ ㉖**. This raw ham has been produced for thousands of years. The curing process takes nine months.

1 Pigs are fed on grains and whey.   2 The meat is salted.

3 The meat is dried.   4 The curing process begins.

5 A layer of lard is added.   6 The curing process is finished.

PIZZA MARGHERITA
Tomato and mozzarella pizza
Preparation: 🕐 45 minutes, baking: 🕐 4×15 minutes, 4×🍕

Pizza dough
- ¾ cup lukewarm water (190 ml)
- 1 pack instant yeast (7 g)
- ½ tsp powdered sugar
- 3¼ cups wheat flour (500 g)
- ½ tsp salt

Sauce
- 2 garlic cloves
- bunch of fresh basil
- 3 tbsp olive oil
- 1 can chopped tomatoes (400 g)
- ½ tsp sugar
- salt and pepper

Toppings
- 250 g mozzarella
- salt and pepper
- olive oil
- fresh basil for garnish

Marco eats pizza nearly every day.

🥖 Pizza dough should be stretched by hand to maintain the bubbles of air that form as the dough rises. With a little practice, anyone can learn to make a perfectly thin and crispy crust, but you can use a rolling pin at first to get you started.

1 Add the yeast and sugar to the water, mix and set aside for a few minutes.

2 Sift the flour and salt into a large bowl. Slowly add the yeast mixture, using a fork to mix. Place your dough on a large flour-dusted surface.

SWEET AND SOUR

▸ Balsamic vinegar is made by fermenting grape juice. It brings out the flavour of cheese, cold cuts, fruit and ice cream.

▸ Authentic balsamic vinegar is only produced in Modena and Reggio Emilia according to an age-old process, which makes it one of the priciest condiments in the world.

▸ Traditional **aceto balsamico** ⑬ is fermented in wooden barrels ④ for at least 12 years, and up to 25 or even more. It is left to mature until it forms a syrupy consistency and it is poured into smaller barrels.

LA DOLCE VITA

▸ There's always room for dessert, isn't there? Of course! Italy has a lot of delicious desserts to choose from.

GELATO ⑤ ⑫

Italian ice cream is served at a slightly warmer temperature so that it is nice and creamy.

CANNOLI ⑧ ⑮

This Sicilian treat is a tube made of deep-fried dough filled with a sweet ricotta filling.

meaning 'cooked cream' in Italian

PANNA COTTA ⑪

A dessert of thick cream served with a drizzle of fruit sauce.

TIRAMISU ⑭

Made of coffee-soaked lady finger biscuits layered with a thick cream of mascarpone beaten with egg yolks.

Italians often enjoy an espresso ⑱* with dessert. It is also served at coffee bars for a quick pick-me-up.

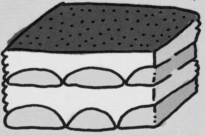

* Discover the history of coffee on page 107.

3 Knead the dough for 10 minutes. Start to stretch the dough, then roll it up into a ball. From time to time, slap the dough against your worktable. When the dough is smooth and elastic, set it aside, sprinkle with flour and cover with a cotton tea towel. Wait 30 minutes — or until it has doubled in size.

4 Chop the garlic and basil. Heat 3 tablespoons of olive oil in a pan, add the garlic and fry for a minute. Add the tomatoes and sugar, and season to taste.

5 Simmer the sauce for 20 minutes, until it thickens and the tomatoes start to fall apart. Add the basil towards the end.

6 Pre-heat your oven to 240°C. Divide your dough into 4 balls. Cover them with a tea towel.

7 Take a ball of dough and stretch it out (but be careful not to make any holes). When it is ready, place on a baking tray covered in baking paper.

Spread 4–5 tablespoons of tomato sauce on top, avoiding the edges. Scatter mozzarella pieces across your pizza. Add salt to taste, drizzle with olive oil and decorate with basil leaves.

8 Bake for 12–15 minutes, until the edges are golden. After you remove the pizza from the oven, add freshly ground pepper and another drizzle of olive oil. Then, do it all again with the rest of your pizza dough!

GREECE
ANCIENT DELIGHTS

MYCENAE

SPARTA

Agamemnon

Homer

Leonidas I

Queen Gorgo

- Ancient Greece had a huge impact on Europe, giving it democracy **8**, philosophy **10**, geometry and other sciences. Greece is where the theatre came to life **11** and, of course, the Olympics!
- Greek cuisine was founded on wheat, olive oil and wine, along with a smattering of vegetables, fruits **16**, cheeses, fish and seafood.
- When Alexander the Great conquered the Persian Empire **12** 2,300 years ago, Persian delicacies flourished in Greece[1]. Later, when the Romans took over **17** and Caesar was in charge **15 19**, Greek kitchens gained lemons, peaches and Indian seasonings **24**.
- Greece eventually became part of the Byzantine Empire[2] **21** and the Ottoman Empire **23**, which is why Greek and Turkish cuisines have a lot in common. In fact, culinary debate still rages over which nation invented tzatziki and moussaka.
- Greece finally regained its independence 200 years ago. Today, it is not only feted for its major contributions to politics, literature and history, but also for its famous feta cheese **1**, fasolada (bean stew) and fava bean dip **2**.

[1] See more about Persia on page 8.
[2] Find out more about Byzantium on page 4.

GIFTS FROM MOUNT OLYMPUS

- The **European olive 5** has been around for 1,000 years.
- An olive branch has long served as a symbol of peace and olive oil was traditionally used as a beauty treatment. Crowns of olive leaves were even placed on the winners' heads at the ancient Olympic Games.
- Many Greeks believed that a plant this precious and useful must be a gift from the gods.

OLIVE OIL PRODUCTION – TRADITIONAL METHO

1 Gather the olives by hand.

2 Remove the leaves and clean.

3 Crush the olives in a mill.

4 Spread the paste onto mats.

5 Press down on the mats.

6 Filter the freshly-squeezed oil.

BIG MASHUP
- The colour and taste of each type of olive depends on its ripeness. All olives need to be soaked in brine to remove the bitter notes and most end up being pressed into olive oil.

AVGOLEMONO SOUP
Chicken broth with egg and lemon
Cooking time (chicken): ⏱ 60 minutes
Preparation: ⏱⏱ 90 minutes, 4×🍲

 4 chicken thighs

 8 cups water (2 l)

 1 cup orzo pasta (190 g) (or uncooked rice)

 3 eggs

 1 lemon

salt and pepper

Avgolemono also refers to a sauce that is often served with meatballs, vegetables, dolma and other warm dishes.

1 Clean the chicken and place in a large pan. Cover with water and add

a teaspoon of salt. Cover and boil for an hour, until the meat is tender and falls off the bone.

2 Take the chicken out of the pot and pick off the meat.

3 Heat the broth to boiling and add the orzo or rice. Cook until soft (10–15 minutes). Set aside.

4 Whisk three eggs together then add the lemon juice and mix.

ATHENS

Socrates and his students

Alexander the Great

Darius III

Augustus

OLIVE OIL PRODUCTION — MODERN METHOD

1 Shake the olives from the trees using a machine.

2 Remove the leaves and clean.

3 A machine crushes the olives into a paste.

4 The olives are spun, drawing out the oil.

5 The filtration process is optional.
(Unfiltered olive oil is considered more premium.)

▶ **Olive oil** ② ⑥ ⑬ ㉒ ㉕ ㉗ can be 'virgin', meaning that the olives were pressed mechanically and without any heat. If less than 24 hours pass between picking the olives and pressing them, the olive oil is deemed 'extra virgin'.

FORGOTTEN FLAVOUR

▶ In ancient times, the seasoning known as **silphium** was key to every feast. Made from a plant that is no longer around today, its roots and stems were used to produce apungent juice similar to asafetida*.

* Find out more about asafetida on page 26.

▶ Silphium was produced in a Greek colony in North Africa. Overcultivation and climate change meant the plant disappeared entirely about 2,000 years ago.

▶ Eating silphium apparently made an animal's meat very tasty so the last of it was probably eaten by a stray cow!

Silphium featured on the money of the local area where it was produced.

5 Gradually add the warm broth to the lemon-egg mixture, stirring constantly with your whisk.

6 When you have added about 4 ladles of broth, pour the whole mixture slowly back into the broth pan, stirring carefully.

7 Season to taste, add some chicken and serve right away.

Stirring is essential to avoid ending up with omelette soup!

Georgios's mum cooked avgolemono every time he had a cold.

Now Georgio cooks it for himself, not only when he is sick!

90

CURDLE SAC

▸ Thanks to traces found in prehistoric Greek vases, we know that people drank cow's milk 8,000 years ago. But when did humans begin making and eating **cheese 1**?

▸ As milk goes off quickly, people probably started making cheese quite early on. Cheesemaking may even have been discovered by accident — if someone left some milk in a sac made of a sheep's stomach.

* Read up on rennet on page 83.

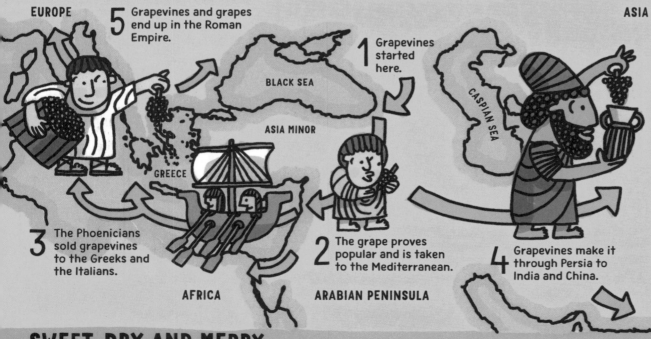

EUROPE

5 Grapevines and grapes end up in the Roman Empire.

1 Grapevines started here.

BLACK SEA

ASIA MINOR

GREECE

ASIA

CASPIAN SEA

3 The Phoenicians sold grapevines to the Greeks and the Italians.

2 The grape proves popular and is taken to the Mediterranean.

4 Grapevines make it through Persia to India and China.

AFRICA

ARABIAN PENINSULA

DIVINE DELIGHTS

▸ Of all the Greek contributions to European arts and philosophy, the finest things to come from Greece are the array of delicious sweet treats, including cakes and biscuits.

▸ It was the Greeks who first came up with the idea of dousing cakes in honey or filling pastry with **sweet cheese 14**. Historical references to sweet Greek treats go back as far as 2,500 years.

SWEET, DRY AND MERRY

▸ For Greeks, the **grapevine 7** is the most precious of plants, alongside the olive, and has just as many uses*.

▸ Grapes can be dried into raisins or pressed into juices and syrups. They can be added to both sweet and savoury dishes.

▸ Grape leaves also come in handy for wrapping meat or rice specialities,

such as dolmades **20 28**, which originated in Turkey.

▸ The grapevine's starring role however is in **wine** production **3 18 26**. Wine was so important to ancient Greeks that it even had its own god, Dionysus. Every Greek banquet included toasts and offerings to their boozy benefactor.

* Read up about balsamic vinegar on page 87.

"Stay away from my cheese!"

CHEESEY POETRY

► The first description of Greek cheesemaking appears in Homer's ❹ epic tale *The Odyssey*. **Homer** tells the story of **Polyphemus** — a giant, man-eating cyclops who apparently liked to wash his human victims down with a piece of cheese.

► The cyclops arrives at his cave, which is full of jars of milk and baskets of maturing cheese. When he spies the humans who have broken into his workshop, he flies into a rage and starts to devour them.

► Did Polyphemus really have a taste for human flesh, or was he was merely attacking the humans to protect his precious store of cheese?

MELOMAKARONA Festive honey biscuits ⏱ 60 minutes, 35–45×●

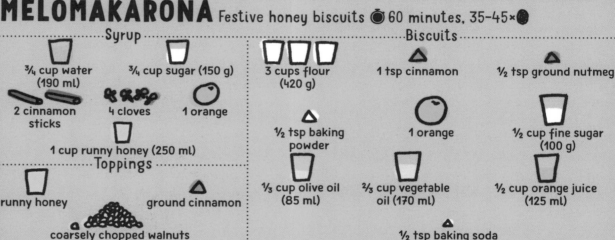

Syrup
- ¾ cup water (190 ml)
- ¾ cup sugar (150 g)
- 2 cinnamon sticks
- 4 cloves
- 1 orange
- 1 cup runny honey (250 ml)

Toppings
- runny honey
- ground cinnamon
- coarsely chopped walnuts

Biscuits
- 3 cups flour (420 g)
- 1 tsp cinnamon
- ½ tsp ground nutmeg
- ½ tsp baking powder
- 1 orange
- ½ cup fine sugar (100 g)
- ⅓ cup olive oil (85 ml)
- ⅔ cup vegetable oil (170 ml)
- ½ cup orange juice (125 ml)
- ½ tsp baking soda

1 Start by making the syrup: place the water, sugar, cinnamon, cloves and orange peel in a pan. Boil for several minutes until the sugar has dissolved. Take the pan off the heat and add the honey. Stir and set aside to cool.

2 Now for the biscuits. In a small bowl, combine the flour with the ground cinnamon, cloves, baking powder, orange peel and sugar. In a second, larger bowl, combine the oils.

3 Add the baking soda to the orange juice and mix until it bubbles. Add the orange juice to the oil blend and mix.

4 Gradually add the flour mixture to the orange-oil blend. Use a spoon to combine the ingredients, then use your hand to knead it together, but not for too long.

5 Heat the oven to 180°C. Shape the biscuits into ovals about 3 cm long.

6 Arrange the biscuits on a greased baking sheet about 2–3 cm apart. Bake for 25 minutes.

7 When cooled, dip the cookies in the honey for 10–15 seconds (do this in batches). Arrange on a plate and sprinkle with walnuts and cinnamon.

Yiayia Maria serves her melomakarona at Christmas.

MOROCCO
FUNNEL OF FLAVOURS

▶ Numerous cultures came together to shape Morocco's rich heritage and cuisine, including the native Berbers of the north and the nomadic Bedouins (accompanied by their camels, sheep and goats). It was ruled by the Roman Empire for 400 years, until the Arabs conquered most of North Africa, and then snatched up by the colonial powers of France and Spain. Morocco didn't gain its independence until 1956.

▶ It is no wonder that this melting pot of influences created a varied cuisine of African, Arabian and Mediterranean flavours: olives ⑭ and olive oil ⑮, wheat breads ❽ ⑱, aromatic soups and fish dishes, fluffy couscous, and pairings of sweet fruits with meat and vegetable dishes ㉔.

▶ Moroccan cuisine is made up of hundreds of unique dishes. It is full of inimitable aromas and unmatched flavour pairings, all washed down with a swig of strong, sweet tea.

ONE FOR THE ROAD

▶ Berbers spent most of their lives travelling, so needed foods that were filling, nutritious, light, easy to prepare and long-lasting.

▶ Couscous fulfils all these requirements. It can be stored for years without losing any of its nutritional content and it requires a lot less water and heat than rice, or any other type of grain.

1
2
3

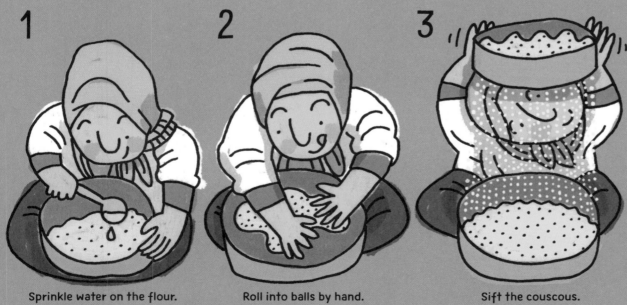

Sprinkle water on the flour.

Roll into balls by hand.

Sift the couscous.

LIGHT AS AIR

▶ Every civilisation has its own methods for quickly filling up a hungry belly[1]. Grain is used to make kasha[2] and porridge, tubers can be boiled or fried, while milled flour can be used to make breads, cakes and pasta. Morocco also has its own starchy staple.

▶ **Couscous ❼** is an essential ingredient in North Africa. The tiny grains are produced by hand, by rolling damp semolina flour into tiny balls.

▶ Steamed couscous is the ideal accompaniment to any main dish or appetizer.

▶ Most couscous is made from wheat, but any type of grain can be used.

[1] Read more about starchy foods on page 102.
[2] Read more about grain dishes on page 64.

DECORATIVE DISHES

▸ **Tagine** ❶ ⓭ ⓳ refers to both the name of Morocco's signature dish and the clay pot used to prepare it.

▸ A tagine is a slow-cooked stew. It can be sweet or sweet-and-savoury thanks to the addition of honey, fruit or nuts.

▸ A tagine is served in the same dish it is cooked in. The cone-shaped lid not only looks good, but keeps the humidity from escaping and allows the stew to simmer.

Tagines are prepared with orange water, pickled lemons and, for special occasions, agarwood crushed with sugar.

A PINCH OF LUXURY

▸ The **agarwood tree** (oud kmari) is the most expensive cooking ingredient in the world and is even pricier than white truffles*.

▸ This luxury item is produced by a tree that is native to Asia. When a particular type of fungus attacks the tree, it releases an aromatic resin. The resin-infused wood is then powdered and used in the production of incense and perfumes — and occasionally added to ceremonial tagines prepared for the most illustrious occasions.

*More about truffles on page 84.

— agar

SEFFA

Sweet couscous ⏱ 30 minutes, 6×🍚

½ cup pitted dates (120 g)

1 cup couscous (200 g)

salt

½ cup milk (125 ml)

¼ cup raisins (40 g)

½ cup hot water (125 ml)

3 tbsp butter (45 g)

¼ cup almonds (40 g)

2 tbsp finely milled sugar

Seffa is usually prepared with a particularly fine type of couscous, but any type you can find will do just fine.

1 Cut the dates into small pieces. Mix the salt into the couscous, along with the dates and raisins. Pour in the milk and set aside for 10 minutes.

2 Then pour the hot water over the mixture, cover and set aside for another 10 minutes.

3 Melt the butter and chop the almonds. Add to the couscous along with the sugar. Try shaping it into a pyramid and sprinkle with cinnamon and the remaining almonds.

Jusef makes the fluffiest seffa in town.

PERFECT PRESENTATION

▸ Close your eyes and imagine a warm sunny day in a splendid garden. Picture yourself standing inside an enormous tent. All around you, there are low tables circled by seas of soft pillows to sit on. Wherever you look, there are wonderfully fragrant dishes: steaming tagines ❶, succulent meats ❷ ⓫ ㉓ and roasted fish ⓬, fluffy pyramids of couscous and aromatic pots of soup ❻ ❾ ⓱. For dessert, a spread of fruits and brightly coloured treats await you ⓾ ⓴. And this is all to be washed down with a perfect pot of sweet tea ❸ ㉒.

▸ This ideally illustrates the scene at a **diffa** ❹ — a Moroccan-style feast which celebrates special occasions.

ORGANIC PROCESS

▸ **Argan oil** is used to make bread, savoury dishes and even desserts ㉕. It is made by pressing the seeds of the **argan tree**, which is native to Morocco and is now a protected species.

▸ For centuries the task of extracting the oil was carried out by women... and goats! Goats loved the taste of argan seeds so much, they climbed into the trees to reach them. The seeds were plucked from the goat's droppings, then cleaned and pressed.

▸ Today, this process has almost entirely been mechanised but women are still in charge and the oil is very popular in the beauty industry.

BASTILLA

A sweet and savoury chicken pie
Cooking time (chicken): ⏱ 1 hour
Preparation: ⏱ 40 minutes
Baking: ⏱ 15 minutes, 6× 🥖

 frozen sheets of filo dough (move from the freezer to the fridge the night before)

2 onions

pinch of saffron

6 tbsp clarified butter (90 g)

1½ kg chicken (preferably thighs)

¾ cup parsely

½ tsp ground ginger

1 tsp ground cinnamon

¼ tsp ground turmeric

1 tsp salt

4 tbsp vegetable oil

2 cups almonds (200 g)

3 tbsp powdered sugar

6 eggs

butter for glazing the filo dough

powdered sugar and cinnamon for sprinkling

SOUR LEMONS

▶ Morocco has a plentiful supply of citrus fruits. Stalls sell freshly squeezed orange or mandarin juice㉑ and enormous jars of **pickled lemons** are everywhere⑯.

▶ The pickling process* gives the lemons an intensely sweet-bitter taste and ensures excess fruit doesn't go to waste. Added to a meal, the lemons bring a unique dash of flavour.

* Read more about pickling on page 65.

1 Slice the lemons part-way down.

2 Heap plenty of salt inside.

3 Stuff the lemons into a jar.

4 Soak with lemon juice.

5 Wait for the lemons to pickle.

Bastilla❺ is traditionally made of warka dough but it's fine to use filo* as a substitute in this recipe.

1 Cut the onion into strips. Dissolve the crushed saffron in two tablespoons of warm water.

2 In a large pan, melt the butter and fry the chicken. Add the onion, parsley, ginger, half the cinnamon, turmeric, saffron water and salt. Add two cups of water and cook on low a heat for 1 hour.

3 Heat the oil in a pan and fry the almonds until browned. Drain on paper towels, cool and then zap in the blender. Mix in the powdered sugar and cinnamon.

4 Remove the chicken from the broth and let it cool. Take the meat off the bone and cut into smaller chunks. Continue reducing the broth until there is around 1½ cups left.

* Read more about the Turkish version of filo dough on page 6.

Whisk the eggs and add to the pot slowly, stirring constantly. Cook for a few minutes longer, until the mixture resembles scrambled eggs. Season to taste.

5 Heat the oven to 220°C. Grease the tin with melted butter and place four sheets of filo at the bottom, so that they fold out over the sides (as shown). Brush each filo sheet with butter.

6 Spread a layer of chicken, then a layer of the egg mixture and top with another two sheets of filo. Brush with butter and sprinkle the almonds on top.

7 Fold the edges of the filo back over the bastilla and cover with the final filo sheet, making sure to tuck it underneath. Brush melted butter over the top. Bake for 15 minutes.

8 Serve hot, decorated with powdered sugar and cinnamon.

Jadda Asma's bastilla is very popular!

EGYPT
BREAKFAST OF PHARAOHS

OLD KINGDOM

1 See more on page 8. 2 Head to page 89. 3 Turn to page 4.

▸ The Egyptian civilisation is among the most ancient in history. The people living along the Nile over 5,000 years ago were united under Narmer, the founder of the first dynasty of pharaohs. The pharaohs ❹ ruled over Egypt for the next 2,500 years and led the construction of the Great Pyramids ❷.

▸ Egypt was invaded by Persia¹, then the Macedonian King Alexander the Great² took over. He established the city of Alexandria ⑫, which swiftly became the main port for the Mediterranean.

▸ For the next 300 years, Egypt was ruled by the Ptolemaic dynasty. When Cleopatra, their last ruler, died the Roman Empire took over ⑬. These lands were then conquered by the Arabs ⑭, the Ottomans ⑮³ and ultimately the British ⑯. Egypt gained its independence in 1956.

▸ The ancient Egyptians left behind awesome architectural structures and inventions.

▸ Today, we know a lot about ancient Egyptian cuisine thanks to archaeological finds. For example, banquets are often shown in paintings from both the Old and New Kingdoms.

HAWAWSHI
Meat-filled pita bread
Preparation: ⏱ 15 minutes
Cooking: ⏱ 40 minutes, 6×◉

◉ Aish baladi is Egypt's most popular traditional bread. Some people bake their own aish baladi, but pita bread is a good substitute.

1 Heat your oven to 180°C. Finely dice the onion, garlic, pepper and parsley. Scald the tomato then peel and cut into chunks. Drain the juice through a strainer.

Farah's children are always happy to have hawawshi for lunch!

IRRIGATION INNOVATION

▸ How was it possible for a nation based in the desert to become such an agricultural superpower? It's all thanks to the Nile — the longest river in all the world. Its source is located far in the south, which sees a great deal of rainfall in summer. Before the invention of dams, the waters of the Nile would rise and inundate its shores. In the autumn, the tide would fall, and the soil left behind was humid and nutrient-rich.

▸ Even 5,000 years ago, the Egyptians had already worked out how to use the annual flooding of the Nile to maximise its irrigation power. They built a system of canals and embankments that allowed them to conserve the excess water and even divert it to fields located further way. This allowed the Egyptians to increase their harvests and protect their cities and villages from flooding at the same time.

Akhenaten

Nefertiti

NEW KINGDOM

Alexander the Great

97

1 onion

1 garlic clove

½ green pepper

a handful of parsley

1 small tomato

500 g ground beef

1 tsp paprika

½ tsp cumin

¼ tsp ground cinnamon

¼ tsp ground ginger

salt and pepper

6 round pitas

50 g butter

2 Use your hands to mix the meat, vegetables and spices together. Season.

3 Cut the pitas along one side to create a pocket and fill it will a medium-sized ball of the meat mix.

4 Spread butter on the top and bottom of the sandwich and wrap in tin foil.

5 Bake for 40 minutes. Cut into two halves and serve.

ESSENTIAL BREAD

▶ Bread 3 has been a staple of the Egyptian diet for over 4,000 years, thanks to farmers who cultivated the grain 1, craftsmen who built the tools to mill the flour and, of course, the millers and bakers 7.

▶ Round, fluffy **aish baladi** 6 19 is a type of popular Egyptian flatbread. It looks similar to a pita, but aish baladi is made with wholegrain flour*. It can be enjoyed on its own, or even with a tasty dish known as ful medames (see more on page 98). It is perfect for mopping up a delicious sauce!

▶ In fact, bread is so important to Egyptian cuisine, it is seen as an essential part of almost every meal. The word 'aish' means 'life', explaining why many Egyptians say 'bread is life'.

* Wholegrain (rye) flour is made by milling the entire grain.

Separate the wheat grains from the chaff.

Remove the hull from the grains.

Grind the flour.

Add water, then knead the dough.

Add a sourdough starter.

Bake!

GASSY HELPERS

▶ What makes bread rise? The ancient Egyptians may have stumbled upon the answer to this question entirely by accident. It's possible that someone used old dough, and instead of getting a flat loaf, they got a puffed-up ball instead!

▶ This fermented dough is called a **sourdough starter** and is still used today. When it's added to raw dough, the bacteria and yeast reproduce , releasing carbon dioxide, which creates lots of tiny air pockets.

▶ This process helps to give sourdough bread its distinct flavour and chewy texture.

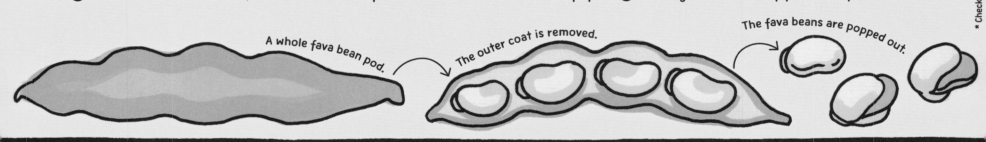

FULL EGYPTIAN BREAKFAST

▸ Many Egyptians start their morning with **ful medames** ⑪⑳ — a hearty bowl of cooked beans.

▸ This rich stew is made of dried fava beans ⑩ that are soaked and then cooked for hours ⑪. It can be cooked with olive oil, butter, egg, sesame paste, meat or vegetables.

▸ Another beany favourite is ta'ameya ⑧⑱ — the Egyptian version of falafel. They are made using dried fava beans, which are then shaped into balls or cakes and deep-fried ⑨.

▸ Ta'ameya spread to the Middle East, where it became known as falafel. Instead of fava beans, chickpeas* became the bean of choice.

▸ These traditional dishes are full of health benefits, as well as being tasty. Beans are a great source of fibre and protein.

* Check out chickpeas on page 15.

A whole fava bean pod.

The outer coat is removed.

The fava beans are popped out.

UMM ALI
Bread pudding
Preparation: ⏱ 15 minutes
Baking: ⏱ 15 minutes, 8 × 🥣

⅔ cup raisins (100 g)

2¾ cups milk (700 ml)

¼ cup sugar (55 g)

1 tsp vanilla extract (optional)

1½ cups double cream (400 ml)

3 tbsp powdered sugar

150 g mixed nuts (e.g. pistachios, almonds, cashews, walnuts)

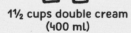
5 croissants

2 tbsp coconut flakes

🥐 Umm Ali ㉒ is a popular dessert made using dry aish baladi or pastry. Old croissants work well!

1 Soak the raisins in warm water and set aside for 15 minutes. Heat he oven to 180°C.

2 Heat the milk, sugar and vanilla in a pan, until it begins to boil. Use a hand mixer to whip the double cream with 1 tablespoon of powdered sugar. Chop the nuts.

TEA DUTY

▸ Black tea ⑰ is the drink of choice in Egypt and is more popular than coffee. People drink it from early in the morning to late into the evening.

▸ Tea is served at all types of gatherings — from casual meet-ups to formal ceremonies — and many Egyptians believe that offering tea to their guests is a duty and not a polite gesture. This is why tea is often referred to as 'wajib', which translates to 'duty' in Arabic.

▸ In Egypt, tea is known as 'shai'.

▸ There are several types of Egyptian tea and infusions:

KOSHARY SHAI

Black tea leaves are steeped in hot water and served with sugar and fresh mint.

SAIDII SHAI

A very strong sweet tea made by boiling the leaves for a long time.

KARKADE

This sweet tea is normally served cold, and is made from hibiscus flowers.

MODERN-DAY CAIRO

TAÄMEYA

BEANS OF LEGEND

▸ In ancient times, cooked fava beans ⑤ were a popular, but also feared food!

▸ Egyptian priests were not allowed to touch the beans, the Romans believed that the souls of the dead were trapped within, while the philosopher Pythagoras forbid his students from eating them.

▸ We don't know the reason for these fears, but the root may be because of a rare genetic disease known as favism*, which is caused by a reaction to eating the beans.

* The words 'fava' and 'favism' come from the Italian word for bean.

'Umm Ali' is Arabic for 'Ali's mum'!

Omar's daughter thinks his desserts are the best!

3 Arrange a layer of croissant pieces in an oven-safe dish about 26 cm across. Sprinkle with the nuts

(saving some for the garnish), raisins and coconut flakes. Add another layer of croissant pieces and pour over the sugary milk.

4 Top with whipped cream and powdered sugar.

5 Bake for 15 minutes. For the last 2 minutes, turn on the grill to brown the top. Sprinkle over the nuts and serve warm.

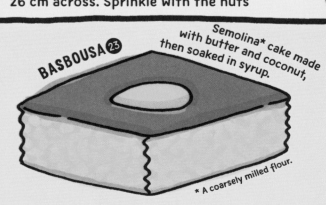

BASBOUSA ㉓

Semolina* cake made with butter and coconut, then soaked in syrup.

* A coarsely milled flour.

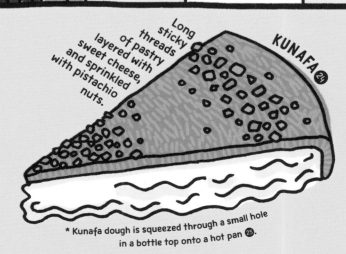

Long sticky threads of pastry layered with sweet cheese, and sprinkled with pistachio nuts.

KUNAFA ㉔

* Kunafa dough is squeezed through a small hole in a bottle top onto a hot pan ㉕.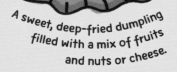

QATAYEF ㉑

A sweet, deep-fried dumpling filled with a mix of fruits and nuts or cheese.

EXTREME SWEETS

▸ Decadent desserts are the perfect finish to a good Egyptian meal.

NIGERIA FUFU FOR ALL

- Nigeria has a long history of different kingdoms and city states. Nigeria's coast also functioned as a major slave-trading post for hundreds of years. This abhorrent practice was developed by Europeans during the colonial period and wasn't abolished until the 20th century.
- Today, Nigeria is among the wealthiest nations in Africa. The country is made up of hundreds of different ethnic tribes and while English is the official language, 500 others are spoken.

- Lagos is the nation's largest city, famous for its nightlife, music scene ⑪ and film industry — known as 'Nollywood' ⑧. More films are produced here than in Hollywood itself!
- Nigerian cuisine has remained resilient in the face of change and Nigerians still relish a bowl of hot red rice and a ball of pounded yams dipped in gravy, just as their ancestors did before them. You would be hard-pressed to find a Nigerian who would turn their nose up at handful of nuts, bursting with caffeine.

STRONG SEEDS
- To add a richness to Nigerian soups, stews and other fish and meat dishes, various vegetable oils are used including palm oil, peanut oil[1], sesame oil[2] and shea butter.

[1] Read more on page 39.
[2] More about sesame on page 15.

NUTTY KOLA
- Kola nuts are seeds which can be chewed or made into a drink. Nigeria produces over half of the world's supply of them!
- The tree that produces kola nuts is related to the cocoa tree*, and it is native to tropical Africa. Kola nuts can be eaten raw, but care needs to be taken — one nut has the same amount of caffeine as two cups of coffee!

*Find out more about cocoa on page 42.

Beneath the white shells lie the fresh seeds.

- In Nigeria, kola nuts are often bought from a street vendor and chewed. They are considered a valuable supplement or even medicine.
- The most famous kola nut product in the world is Coca-Cola®, which was invented over 100 years ago. The original recipe was devised by an American pharmacist named John Pemberton.

- **Palm oil** is made of the fruits ② of the tropical oil palm (*Elaeis guineensis*). To make palm oil, either just the seeds are pressed ⑦, producing a yellowish oil, or the entire nut (producing an intensely red oil).
- The oil is used to make margarine and other spreads and can be used for frying. It is even used as an ingredient in fuel and in the cosmetics industry. The development of palm oil on a mass scale has however led to widespread deforestation, so many people are trying to reduce its production and consumption.

1

Separate the pulp.

2

Boil the nuts.

3

Remove the shells.

4
Allow to dry.

5

Crush the nuts.

6
Roast.

7

Grind the roasted nuts.

8
Add some water.

9

Separate the shea butter.

10
Heat to remove impurities.

11

Filter the shea butter.

12
The butter is ready!

▶ **Shea butter 5** is made from the nuts of the shea tree (*Vitellaria paradoxa*). It's used in cooking and to make soaps, candles and creams.

GROUNDNUT SOUP
Nutty chicken stew*
⏱ 1.5 hours, 6×🍚

🍗 You can use any type of meat to make this soup* or replace with potato and root vegetables.

1 Heat the oil and butter in a deep frying pan. Add the chicken and flash fry it on both sides.

2 Add the water, laurel leaves and salt. Cover and simmer for about 45 minutes, until the chicken is tender.

3 Roast the nuts in a hot, dry pan. When they are golden, let them cool and then blend into a paste (if you are not using peanut butter).

4 Blend the onion, garlic, chilli and tomatoes — but not too finely.

5 Ladle the meat out of the pot. Add the groundnut paste, the tomato-onion blend and oil. Cook for 10-15 minutes, stirring from time to time.

6 Put the chicken back in the pot, add the spinach and cook for a few minutes. Serve with rice.

* Nigerian soups are more like a stew or sauce.

 4 tbsp vegetable oil
1 tbsp clarified butter
 1½ kg chicken pieces

 2 cups water (500 ml)
2 laurel leaves
1 tbsp salt

1½ shelled peanuts (200 g) or 1 cup peanut butter (240 g)
2 small red onions

 2 cloves of garlic
½ fresh chilli pepper
3 small tomatoes or 1 can (400 g)

 2 tbsp palm oil (or other vegetable oil)
a handful of fresh spinach (or you can use frozen spinach)
 rice (to serve)

Samuel loves to cook for his family.

LAGOS

JOLLOF 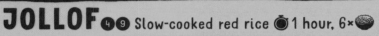 Slow-cooked red rice ⏱ 1 hour, 6× 🍽

 2 cups long-grain rice (like basmati) (400 g)

2 small red onions

 4 medium tomatoes or 2 cans chopped tomatoes (400 g each)

2 cloves garlic

1 chilli pepper

1 red pepper

2 tbsp palm (or other) oil

3 tbsp tomato puree

3 cups stock or water (750 mL)

△ 2 tsp salt

△ 1 tsp dried thyme

△ ½ tsp ground ginger

△ ½ tsp cumin

△ ½ tsp pepper

Esther's jollof rice is a hit!

1 Rinse the rice thoroughly. Chop 1 red onion and blend the other (coarsely) with the tomatoes, garlic, chilli and paprika.

2 Fry the chopped onion in oil for a few minutes, then add the tomato puree and cook for another 2 minutes. Then add the tomato-onion blend. Cover and simmer for 15 minutes.

3 Add the salt and seasonings, then the rice and water (or stock). Mix well. Cover and simmer on a low heat for 15–20 minutes, or until the liquid has evaporated. If the rice is still too firm, add a bit of water and simmer for another 5 minutes.

4 Let the rice settle for 15 minutes, then serve.

STAR STARCHES

▸ The basic desire to feel full and satisfied has always driven humans to find nutritious and filling food. Every civilisation on Earth has found their own local source of starch — a type of complex carbohydrate that is metabolised slowly and keeps the belly feeling fuller for longer.

▸ Popular starches include various grains, beans, tubers and other root vegetables.

▸ It's clear from this book just how important starchy foods are to local cuisines around the world: from wheat bread in Egypt, rye bread in Germany and rice in China and Japan, as well as kasha in Poland, cassava in Brazil and many types of noodles and dumplings from the Far East to Western Europe and beyond.

▸ Nigeria's star starches are:

TARO

RICE

YAM

SORGHUM

MILLET

PLANTAINS

CASSAVA

MINE'S BETTER

▸ African varieties of rice were domesticated independently from their Asian cousins. Today, all kinds of rice are popular.
▸ Rice is the main ingredient in jollof ④ ⑨. Its intense orange colour comes from palm oil and tomatoes.
▸ There are many different types of jollof rice and Nigerians, Senegalese and Ghanaians all argue about whose jollof came first and which is the best.

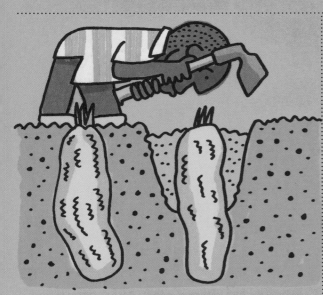

BIGGEST OF THE BUNCH

▸ The massive yam ① — which can reach as much as 20 kg in weight — is an integral part of daily life in Nigeria.
▸ Yams require quite a lot of water to grow so they are usually harvested after the rainy season.
▸ The harvest period is also a time of celebration, with the yam starring as the guest of honour.

1

Peel the yams.

2

Boil in hot water.

3

Pound the yams.

4

Knead and shape.

5

The yam balls are ready!

6

They can be enjoyed with lots of dishes.

YUMMY YAMS

▸ Yams are typically pounded ③ ⑥ ⑩ until they form a single ball of goodness.
▸ The yams are boiled before they are pounded. There is a powdered form, however, which just requires water.

▸ Pounded yam doesn't have any flavour of its own, so it is the perfect accompaniment to spicy dishes. It is traditionally eaten by tearing off a piece by hand and using it to scoop up a stew or sauce. In many African countries, this type of starchy ball is often called 'fufu'.

ETHIOPIA
THICK, BUTTERY, SOUR AND SPICY

▶ The earliest traces of human activity in Ethiopia date back over 200,000 years. The ancient city of Aksum, which stood here for 1,000 years, had a powerful empire. Despite many attempts from other regimes to conquer the nation, Ethiopia has stayed largely independent. Its main challenge however has always been the harsh climate and the long-lasting dry spell which means just three months of rainfall ❸ each year.

▶ With the rainy season comes luscious green fields. The harvest needs to be gathered quickly, and historically the provisions had to last the entire year. A failed harvest was catastrophic, as Ethiopian people would be at risk of starvation, or even death.

▶ Close ties with tradition and mistrust of outside influences, alongside harsh conditions, created a simple but distinctive cuisine. At the heart of every Ethiopian meal is a traditional fermented flatbread, aromatic clarified butter and a range of hearty meat and vegetable stews.

SOURDOUGH STAPLE

▶ Injera ❺ is a thin, pan-fried flatbread made of teff flour. Teff ❶ is native to Ethiopia and is its most important foodstuff. The fermenting process gives injera its sour kick.

▶ Ethiopia is known for its thick stews, served on top of an injera. To enjoy, diners use their hands to scoop up a piece of injera with the stew ❷. There's no need for a knife or fork!

▶ Typically, a whole table of people shares a single dish, so licking your fingers is forbidden (and you must wash your hands before sitting down!).

1 Mix flour and water together.

2 Allow to ferment.

3 Spread the dough on a hot pan.

4 Fry.

Injera is a symbol of good fortune, so Ethiopians often say:

> May injera come to you!

CLASSIC INJERA
Flatbread
Fermentation: 2–3 days
Preparation: ⏱ 20 minutes, 7 × 🥞

1 cup brown teff flour (160 g)

1 cup wheat flour (150 g)

2½ cups lukewarm water (625 ml)

¾ tsp salt

clarified butter

Injera's sour flavour is due to the fermentation process of the dough but if you're in a hurry, try the express version on the righthand page.

Dauit's injera starter is ready!

1 Take a large glass jar and add both types of flour. Add water and mix. The mixture should be thick but still runny (add more flour or water if needed).

2 Cover the jar with a tea towel and set aside for 2–3 days, mixing as often as you can.

3 When fermentation is complete, the mixture should have a slightly sour smell and bubbles should appear when mixed.

JUST FOR YOU

▸ No matter where in the world you go, eating a meal together is an act of hospitality and kinship. In Ethiopia, this is expressed through the gesture of kindness known as **gursha**.

▸ When friends and family get together over a plate of injera, one person prepares a gursha (meaning 'mouthful') of injera and stew to serve to the person sitting beside them.

ALICHA   KITFO

WAT

FRAGRANT BUTTER

▸ The other Ethiopian must-have is **niter kibbeh*** (also spelled nit'ir qibe) — clarified butter with herbs such as cumin, cardamom, fenugreek, cinnamon, nutmeg or ginger. The milk solids are drained off, leaving behind a golden tub of pure fat that can be used in cooking. It last for many months — even up to a whole year.

* Similar to ghee — described on page 25.

HEARTY AND SPICY

▸ A plate of injera is loaded with various sauces and condiments.

▸ **Wat** refers to a spicy dish, typically prepared with a chilli ❽ and spice mix known as **berbere** ❾. **Alicha** ❿ dishes are milder.

▸ **Kitfo** is a traditional type of beef tartar seasoned with an aromatic dash of niter kibbeh.

4 Add salt to the mixture just before frying and stir.

5 Heat clarified butter in a pan and spread out an even layer of dough. When the top starts to get crispy, cover the pan and cook for another minute. Continue until you've used up all your dough.

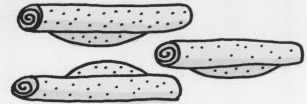

INJERA EXPRESS

⏱ 20 minutes, 4×◉

½ cup teff flour (80 g)   ½ cup rye flour (75 g)   ½ tsp baking soda

½ tsp salt   1 cup water (250 ml)   3 tsp yoghurt   1 tsp vinegar

🥄 In a large bowl, combine the two types of flour, baking soda and salt. Add the water, yoghurt and vinegar until smooth. Fry as per the main recipe.

Menelik II

DORO WAT

Stew with chicken and eggs

2 hours, 6×

1½ kg chicken pieces (no skin)

10 large red onions

6 tbsp clarified butter (80 g)

3 garlic cloves

3 cm ginger stem

⅓ tbsp berbere

1 tbsp honey

6 eggs

salt

Doro wat is traditionally made with **niter kibbeh**, but you can use ghee or your own clarified butter instead.

1 Place the chicken in a large bowl and cover with water. Coarsely chop the red onions.

2 Melt half the butter in a deep pan and cook the onion on a low heat and cover for 30 minutes, stirring occasionally.

3 Add the rest of the butter, the berbere seasoning, chopped garlic and ginger. Cook for another 30 minutes.

4 Add the chicken, honey and a teaspoon of salt. Add a bit of water to ensure the meat is covered. Cover and cook for an hour, until the chicken is tender.

5 Hard boil the eggs, peel and poke them with a knife. Add them to the pot and cook for a few more minutes. Season to taste and serve with injera*.

* Find the injera recipe on the previous page.

FIT FOR AN EMPRESS

▶ More than 130 years ago, Empress Taytu Betul decided to host the party of the century ⑪ in order to celebrate Ethiopia's new capital **Addis Ababa** (which translates to 'new flower') and to show off Ethiopian culture to the world.

▶ The party was a great success. A giant tent was set up with 1,000 baskets of injera ⑫.

Jars of butter, seasonings and sauces filled the room along with plenty of meat stews. A total of 5,395 sheep and goats were slaughtered for the great feast!

▶ The empress even cooked some of the dishes herself. The food served that night went down in history and set the foundation for Ethiopian cuisine.

A BANANA BUT NOT REALLY

▶ **Ensete** ⑦ is the Egyptian version of a banana — except that the fruit is inedible. Instead, the plant's roots and pulp are eaten. A single plant can provide as much as 40 kg of **kocho** — a sweet pulp that can be boiled, baked or made into a drink.

1 Chop the root.

2 Scrape off the pulp.

3 Ferment the pulp.

4 Cook!

Tuytu Betul

Zala's doro wat is perfect for cosy family dinners.

BERBERE

Spice mixture ⏱ 10 minutes, 1× 🍲

4 cardamom pods

1 tsp fenugreek seeds

1 tsp coriander seeds

1 tsp peppercorns

3 cloves

⅓ cup dried chillies

2 tbsp sweet paprika powder

1 tsp ground ginger

¼ tsp ground cinnamon

¼ tsp ground nutmeg

1 tsp salt

1. Shell the cardamom and dry roast the seeds together with the fenugreek and coriander seeds, pepper and cloves. When cool, zap in a blender.

2. Add the rest of the seasonings and zap again. Berbere can be stored in a sealed jar for about 3 months.

An Ethiopian shepherd apparently noticed his goats were more alert after eating the fruits of a coffee plant.

Islamic mystics (sufis) drank coffee before a night of prayers.
(Over 7,000 years ago.)

Sufis from Yemen came up with the idea of roasting and grinding coffee beans.
(About 6,000 years ago.)

Syrian traders bring coffee to Turkey.
(Over 400 years ago.)

A Polish nobleman called Jerzy Franciszek Kulczycki set up one of the first coffee shops in Vienna.
(Over 300 years ago.)

In Paris over 27,000 cafés open up to meet the demand for coffee.
(Over 100 years ago.)

LUXURY FOR ALL

▸ **Coffee** is a stimulant*. It is made from the fruits of trees and shrubs native to Ethiopia. The mature coffee beans are dried in the sun 6, roasted, ground and brewed.

▸ No one knows exactly when humans first discovered the effects of coffee.

* Coffee contains caffeine, which has a stimulating effect on the brain.

▸ At first, the raw beans were chewed, or the shells brewed into a drink. Arab traders realised the potential and began transporting coffee through the Middle East.

▸ Coffee became popular in Europe later. At first, it was treated as a medicine, and drunk when someone needed to be 'perked up'. Soon enough, the flavour also became popular.

Today, coffee is drunk all over the world, with the greatest number of coffee drinkers in the north of Europe. Scandinavians tend to drink an average of three cups per day!

▸ From Europe, coffee then made it to the colonies in the Americas and Asia. It was discovered anew in Ethiopia and is the nation's number one export product.

FOODIE TIMELINE

Certain dates are approximations — not every historical event can be located in time with absolute certainty.

300,000 YEARS AGO
Earliest traces of Homo sapiens

13,500 YEARS AGO

Rice domesticated in Asia
19

Millet domesticated in Asia
64

First signs of wheat cultivation in the Fertile Crescent of the Middle East
6

Figs are domesticated in the Middle East
15

Chickpeas domesticated
15

Start of sugar cane cultivation in Asia
27

The oldest traces of milk residue in clay pots
90

The chicken's ancestors are domesticated in Southeast Asia
33

| 11,500 BCE | 11,100 BCE | 10,700 BCE | 10,300 BCE | 9,900 BCE | 9,500 BCE | 9,100 BCE | 8,700 BCE | 8,300 BCE | 7,900 BCE | 7,500 BCE | 7,100 BCE | 6,700 BCE | 6,30... |

Earliest references to honey and sweet cheese pastries in Greece
90

Nazca lines appear in the plains of Peru
44

King Leonidas and Queen Gorgo rule over Sparta
88

Socrates starts to philosophise
89

Mayan pyramid is built in Calakmul
40

Garum fish sauce is popularised in the Mediterranean region
5

Alexander the Great conquers Persia and Egypt
88, 96

City of Alexandria is founded
96

Europeans begin cultivating beetroot
71

Chinese create their own fish sauce
28

China invades the ancient empire of Vietnam
28

Soy sauce and miso are popularised in China
21, 23

Jews regain control of the temple in Jerusalem
14

Start of cabbage cultivation in Europe
71

The Romans take over Greece
88

Cleopatra becomes the ruler of Egypt
96

Augustus conquers Egypt
96

The start of the Roman Empire
84

Augustus is head of the Roman Empire
88

Augustus discovers his love of asparagus
63

The demise of sylphium
89

Pliny the Elder applauds the fine attributes of black swine in his *'Natural History'*
77

The first type of sugar manufactured in India
27

Romans expel the Jews from Jerusalem
12

Kingdom of Aksum established in Ethopia as the most powerful in the region
104

The Roman Emperor Constantine the Great moves the capital to
4

Roman Emperor Constantine the Great establishes a 'New Rome' in Byzantium
90

| 500 BCE | 400 BCE | 300 BCE | 200 BCE | 100 BCE | 0 | 100 | 200 | 3... |

109

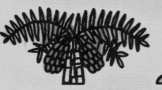

Date palms are domesticated in the Middle East
11

The Indus Valley Civilisation develops in South Asia
24

First olive harvests on the Mediterranean coast
88

China discovers tea
16

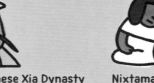

The first Chinese Xia Dynasty is established
16

Nixtamalization of corn is developed in South America
40

The kingdoms of Israel and Judea are founded
12

Homer writes *The Odyssey*, including the first description of ancient cheesemaking
91

Pistachios are eaten in the region that is Iran today
10

The ancient people of Peru start raising llamas and alpacas
44

Sesame is domesticated in India
15

The lands of Egypt are unified into a single kingdom
96

The Egyptians develop a technique to use the Nile for irrigation
96

The first Egyptian pyramids are built
96

The start of wine-growing in the Mediterranean region
90

The beginning of the Mayan civilisation
40

The kingdoms of Israel and Judea are founded
12

Rice is domesticated in Africa
103

Persivan invasion of Egypt
96

City of Bizantium is founded
4

The native people of South America start eating potatoes
46

The Norte Chico people construct the most ancient city in America. An advanced civilisation develops in the Andes
44

Popcorn is eaten by the native people of today's Mexico
36

Pomegranates are domesticated in the Middle East
8

Almonds are domesticated in the Middle East
10

The cultivation of roses begins in the Middle East
9

Saffron is widely known in Iran
9

Turnips start to be cultivated in Europe
71

Solon introduces early democratic practices in Greece
88

King Nebuchadnezzar II of the Babylonian Empire conquers the kingdom of Judea
12

Cyrus II establishes the Persian Empire
8

| 5,500 BCE | 5,100 BCE | 4,700 BCE | 4,300 BCE | 3,900 BCE | 3,500 BCE | 3,100 BCE | 2,700 BCE | 2,300 BCE | 1,900 BCE | 1,500 BCE | 1,100 BCE | 700 BCE |

Mayan civilisation flourishes
40

Buddhism becomes the national religion in Japan
21

The tagine is developed in the Middle East and North Africa
93

Vikings attack and take over the territory of today's Norway
56

Kingdom of Nri is established in Nigeria
100

People living in what is Russia today start brewing kvass
70

People of the Byzantine Empire start eating caviar
5

Turkish nomads learn to bake bread in a pot
6

Fall of the Roman Empire
84

Arab invaders take over Morocco
92

Arab invaders taken over Egypt
96

First mention of narezushi in Japanese records
22

Chinese tea master Lu Yu writes his famous treatise on the beverage
16

Mayans construct the Kukulcán Temple
40

Wheat-based halva is popularised
7

Arab traders bring rice to Spain
76

Italians start curing prosciutto crudo
86

In North Africa, women start pressing oil out of argan seeds
94

German tribes invade the Iberian Peninsula
76

Germans start to brew beer on the Iberian Peninsula
76

Arab invaders arrive in the Iberian peninsula, taking over the lands but also bringing in new food products
76

Wasabi is popularised as a condiment in Japan
23

First reports of ergotism symptoms — an extreme reaction to spoiled rye
61

The first kissels are made near Kiev during an enemy invasion
70

Mieszko I becomes the first king of Poland
64

Stephen I, King of Hungary, introduces Christianity
72

Leif Eriksson (probably) sails all the way to North America
56

The Incan Empire rises and its people start making Chuño and drink chicha morada
44, 47

| 400 | 500 | 600 | 700 | 800 | 900 | 1000 | 1100 | 1200 |

110

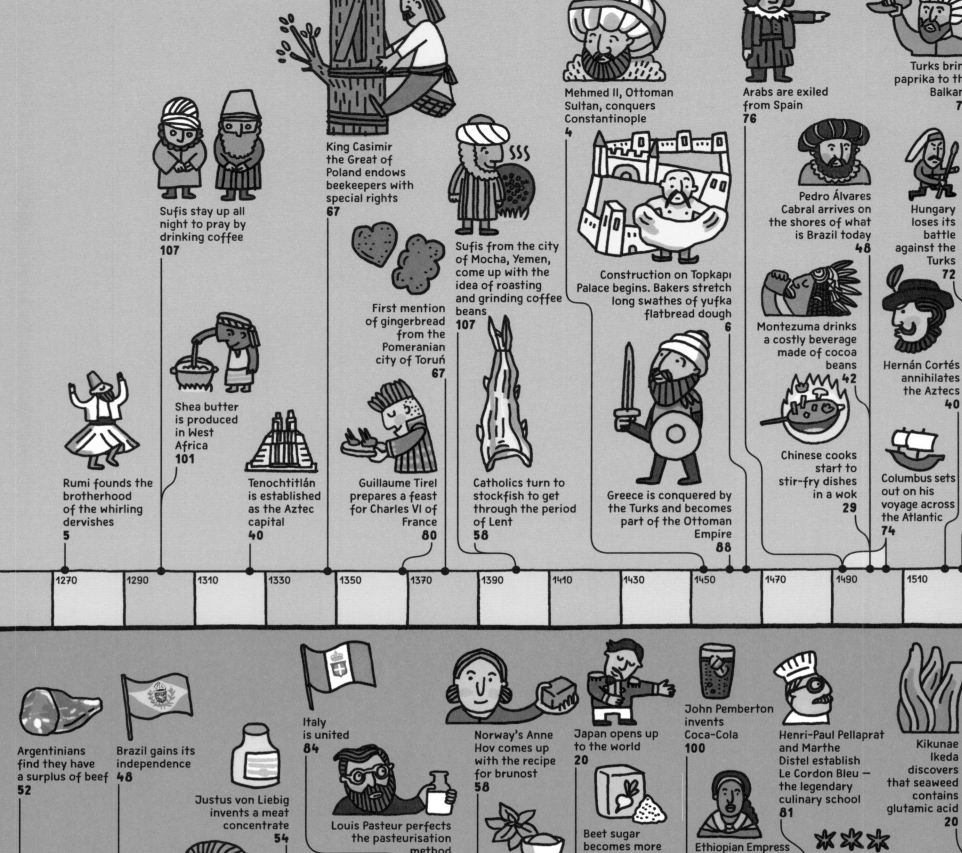

Rumi founds the brotherhood of the whirling dervishes
5

Sufis stay up all night to pray by drinking coffee
107

Shea butter is produced in West Africa
101

Tenochtitlán is established as the Aztec capital
40

King Casimir the Great of Poland endows beekeepers with special rights
67

First mention of gingerbread from the Pomeranian city of Toruń
67

Guillaume Tirel prepares a feast for Charles VI of France
80

Sufis from the city of Mocha, Yemen, come up with the idea of roasting and grinding coffee beans
107

Catholics turn to stockfish to get through the period of Lent
58

Mehmed II, Ottoman Sultan, conquers Constantinople
4

Construction on Topkapı Palace begins. Bakers stretch long swathes of yufka flatbread dough
6

Greece is conquered by the Turks and becomes part of the Ottoman Empire
88

Arabs are exiled from Spain
76

Pedro Álvares Cabral arrives on the shores of what is Brazil today
48

Montezuma drinks a costly beverage made of cocoa beans
42

Chinese cooks start to stir-fry dishes in a wok
29

Turks bring paprika to the Balkans
74

Hungary loses its battle against the Turks
72

Hernán Cortés annihilates the Aztecs
40

Columbus sets out on his voyage across the Atlantic
74

1270 1290 1310 1330 1350 1370 1390 1410 1430 1450 1470 1490 1510

Argentinians find they have a surplus of beef
52

Brazil gains its independence
48

Justus von Liebig invents a meat concentrate
54

Italy is united
84

Louis Pasteur perfects the pasteurisation method
83

Norway's Anne Hov comes up with the recipe for brunost
58

First mention of basil pesto on record
85

Japan opens up to the world
20

Beet sugar becomes more and more popular
27

John Pemberton invents Coca-Cola
100

Ethiopian Empress Taytu Betul hosts the feast of a lifetime
106

Henri-Paul Pellaprat and Marthe Distel establish Le Cordon Bleu — the legendary culinary school
81

The first Michelin Guide is published
80

Kikunae Ikeda discovers that seaweed contains glutamic acid
20

The Japanese start making nigirizushi
22

Anthelme Brillat-Savarin enjoys eating well and writing essays on his foodie escapades
80

Chocolate bars are produced in the United Kingdom
42

Norway begins mass-producing tins of sardines
59

Creation of the Imperial State of Germany
60

The first margherita pizzas are made in Italy
84

Fortune cookies appear in the U.S.
37

Paprika becomes Hungary's favourite seasoning
75

Marie-Antoine Carême launches a widespread appreciation for haute cuisine
81

White sausage is popularised in Germany
62

Chop suey appears in the U.S.
37

The Austro-Hungarian Empire is founded
71

Vietnam is made a colony of France
28

The British take control of Egypt
96

Spanish bars start serving tapas
79

Georges August Escoffier comes up with the brigade system of organising work in the kitchen
80

Phở broths become popular in Vietnam
29

1820 1830 1840 1850 1860 1870 1880 1890 1900 1910

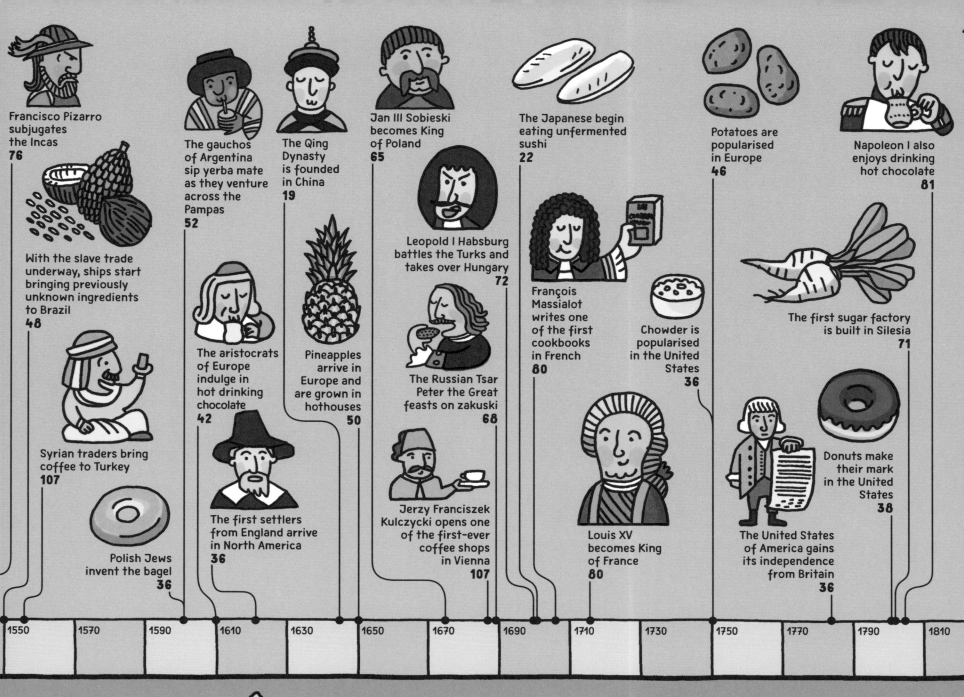

Francisco Pizarro subjugates the Incas
76

The gauchos of Argentina sip yerba mate as they venture across the Pampas
52

The Qing Dynasty is founded in China
19

Jan III Sobieski becomes King of Poland
65

The Japanese begin eating unfermented sushi
22

Potatoes are popularised in Europe
46

Napoleon I also enjoys drinking hot chocolate
81

With the slave trade underway, ships start bringing previously unknown ingredients to Brazil
48

The aristocrats of Europe indulge in hot drinking chocolate
42

Pineapples arrive in Europe and are grown in hothouses
50

Leopold I Habsburg battles the Turks and takes over Hungary
72

The Russian Tsar Peter the Great feasts on zakuski
68

François Massialot writes one of the first cookbooks in French
80

Chowder is popularised in the United States
36

The first sugar factory is built in Silesia
71

Syrian traders bring coffee to Turkey
107

The first settlers from England arrive in North America
36

Jerzy Franciszek Kulczycki opens one of the first-ever coffee shops in Vienna
107

Louis XV becomes King of France
80

The United States of America gains its independence from Britain
36

Donuts make their mark in the United States
38

Polish Jews invent the bagel
36

1550 1570 1590 1610 1630 1650 1670 1690 1710 1730 1750 1770 1790 1810

The first kibbutzes in Palestine
15

Hungary begins cultivating red peppers for paprika production
75

Argentina becomes the world's biggest producer of yerba mate
55

Kathleen Drew solves the nori mystery in Japan
21

Tiramisu becomes a popular dessert in Italy
87

Astronauts enjoy quinoa up on the ISS
47

Nathan Handwerker opens the first hot dog shop in Coney Island
38

The first popcorn machine is installed in the U.S.
36

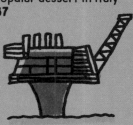
Petroleum reserves are discovered in Norwegian waters
56

George Washington Carver promotes peanuts among Americans
39

White Castle opens in the U.S. as the first fast-food restaurant
37

Egypt gains its independence
96

The first Turkish kebab shop opens in Germany
5

Astronauts start cultivating amaranth grain in space and baking amaranth cookies
47

The first Michelin stars are awarded
80

Israel is declared a country
12

Herta Charlotte Heuwer serves the first currywurst in Germany
62

Morocco regains its independence
92

1930 1940 1950 1960 1970 1980 1990 2000 2010 2020

INDEX